REFORMERS AND VISIONARIES

The Americanization of
The Art of Dance

Nancy Lee Chalfa Ruyter

REFORMERS AND

VISIONARIES

The Americanization of
the Art of
Dance

DANCE HORIZONS, NEW YORK : 1979

ISBN 0-87127-101-X

Library of Congress Catalog card number: 77-81990

Printed in the United States of America

Dance Horizons, 1801 East 26th Street, Brooklyn, N.Y. 11229

TO

MY MOTHER

Lois S. McClary

AND

MY FATHER

Andrew B. Chalfa

Contents

Part I.
The Theatrical Dance Tradition in America

Part II.
The Educational Dance Tradition in America

Appendixes

Illustrations

Acknowledgments

I am indebted to Christena L. Schlundt of the University of California at Riverside, who stimulated and nurtured my early interest in dance history. It was largely as a result of initial studies with her that I took my degrees in history and committed myself to dance. Professor Schlundt also served on my dissertation committee at Claremont Graduate School, where the first version of this book was written. She and the other committee members—John Niven (Chairman), Leonard Pronko, and Edward White—all offered valuable comments and suggestions.

For assistance in my research for this study I am grateful to the staff of The New York Public Library Dance and Theatre Collections and to Helen Hardy of the Honnold Library of the Claremont Colleges. I am also indebted to The New York Public Library and to the State Historical Society of Wisconsin for permission to reproduce photographs from their collections. Thanks are due to Frank Derbas for copying pictures from The New York Public Library, to Doris Hering for her perceptive and thought-provoking critique of the original manuscript, and to Dorothy Macdonald for skillful editing of the final revision.

Thanks to the *American Dance Guild Newsletter*, which carried my request for information and reminiscences about Margaret H'Doubler and Gertrude Colby, I received responses from: Ruth L. Murray, Anna Halprin, Harriet Smith Mason, Adelin Linton, Mary Jane Wolbers, Mary H. Kaprelian, Lonny Joseph Gordon, Stella Moore, and Florence Price. Their contributions were a great help to me, and I am in their debt. In particular, Florence Price made thoughtful and valuable suggestions and helped in arranging a meeting with Margaret H'Doubler. I proffer the warmest thanks to Miss H'Doubler and Mrs. Price for the delightful and informative meeting that we had.

Ellen Moore of Madison, Wisconsin made a painstaking search for early photographs of Miss H'Doubler and provided me with some materials I had not been able to find elsewhere.

Finally, my thanks to my husband, Hans C. Ruyter, for his many suggestions and help in preparing the manuscript.

A Note on Documentation

The data upon which this study is based has been taken from the works listed in the bibliography. For the most part, however, sources have been specified only for direct quotations. Any reader interested in the detailed and extensive original documentation may consult the dissertation of the same title (Claremont Graduate School, 1970). It is in the Honnold Library of the Claremont Colleges and on file with University Microfilms.

Introduction

This is a study of the way dance as an art acquired a respected place in American middle-class culture. The role of dance in eighteenth and nineteenth century American society will be looked at first for a better understanding of advances that were made in the twentieth century. It will be seen that dance had to lose its aristocratic and formal character and to align itself with more democratic, progressive, middle-class American values and aspirations before it could be taken seriously by the American people.

Dance is often considered a nonintellectual activity, and perhaps it has been that in many of its forms. But the new dance that developed in America—beginning with the work of Isadora Duncan and Ruth St. Denis and continuing to the present day—has been self-consciously intellectual from the beginning. American dance innovators studied history, philosophy, art history, and religion in order to bring dance to the standard of the other arts and shape it in terms of such models. They were striving to create a dance art that could be accepted in the pantheon of the fine arts.

More than anything else, these pages are an intellectual history of modern American dance in its first flowering. The story has two parts: dance as it developed in theater and dance as it was used in education. These two developments were separate until the twentieth century, because our eighteenth and nineteenth century forebears made a sharp distinction between theatrical dance on the one hand and social or educational dance forms on the other. Even though respectable people enjoyed attending dance performances—provided that they were in good taste—the same people had no respect for the profession of theatrical dance. Professional dancers were looked down upon, and no proper person would dance on a stage either as an amateur or as a professional. In contrast, social and educational dance forms have been integrated into American society from the beginning and practiced by the "best" people as well as the worst.

It would be well at the start to note the difference between theatrical dance and social dance since they cannot always be distinguished on the basis of the type of dance performed in each context. For example, folk and ballroom dance—two social forms—have often been theatricalized and presented on the stage. The difference lies in the main purpose of each as a social institution and in the characteristic way in which each is organized.

Theatrical dance is performed primarily for the pleasure and amusement of an audience that observes but does not participate. Social dance, on the other hand, is typified by the pleasures and benefits derived from it by the dancers themselves. While theatrical dance in eighteenth and nineteenth century America had no social function beyond entertainment, social dance offered two kinds of benefits. On the personal level it provided pleasure, recreation, and an attractive means of social intercourse. On the educational level it was a source of healthful exercise as well as a means of teaching grace, manners, and a sense of form—accomplishments highly valued by society.

The first dances used as education in America were social dances. In contrast, the dance genre that was developed for educational purposes in the twentieth century began as theatrical dancing. Only after the earliest pioneers of the new dance had established it as an art form for the stage was it incorporated into educational programs. Since then, modern dance has been offered in schools both for personal growth and development and for presentation in public performances.

These two developments and how they merged are the subject of the pages that follow. The historical background of theatrical dance in America leads to the ideas and aspirations of the twentieth century theatrical dance innovators. From this we come to dance in American education, from its historical background in colonial times to the use of modern forms as an instrument of education. With the entrance of the new dance into the schools, dance as a theatrical art had finally won a measure of acceptance in American society. It had come a long way in a few decades.

PART I:
The Theatrical Dance Tradition in America

Above: Carte de visite showing corps de ballet of *The Black Crook*. (Dance Collection, The New York Public Library at Lincoln Center.) Below: "Grand Ballet of Arts and Sciences" from Imre Kiralfy's historical spectacle, *America*, opening in Chicago in 1893. (From program in Dance Collection, The New York Public Library at Lincoln Center.)

CHAPTER 1

Dance in Theater:
The Eighteenth and
Nineteenth Centuries

Dance as a professional performing art has received relatively little attention in studies of pre-twentieth century American cultural history. Nevertheless, what can be gleaned from a few general histories and a growing number of monographs shows that theatrical dance has been more prominent in American culture since colonial times than we have been led to believe.

Much has been made of Puritan antagonism to the arts and entertainment in the early history of the colonies. It has also been shown that such antagonism was neither as rigid nor as pervasive as was once imagined. Moral disapproval of dance and theater is a continuing theme in America until well into the twentieth century, but no one has yet shown that a stern harangue from the pulpit has lowered the box office receipts for any theatrical productions—although such disapproval has undoubtedly kept respectable people out of the theatrical professions. But one need not hold the Puritans responsible for the lack of theatrical activity in the early years of the American colonies. If there had been no Puritans, there still would have been no theaters because there were no cities. As the historian Louis B. Wright has pointed out, "stage plays, concerts, opera, and all such formal and sophisticated entertainment require a settled urban life to support them."[1] Moral scruples, combined with the lack of cities, postponed the development of professional performing arts in colonial America.

By the early decades of the eighteenth century, cities had grown wealthy enough and moral scruples lax enough that a few theaters were built and tolerated. Almost from the beginning, dancing was performed on the stages of these theaters. The first colonial theater of which there is record was completed in 1718 in Williamsburg, Virginia. Two of its promoters, Charles and Mary Stagg, put on plays in which they performed as actors and dancers, taught dancing, and organized public balls and assemblies. A third partner in the enterprise served as casting agent, engaging performers from England to play in the productions. By the 1740s theaters or buildings temporarily converted to theatrical use were available in New York, Philadelphia, and Charleston, and professional performing troupes were touring the colonies.

From announcements and news of current dance attractions in newspapers and playbills of the second half of the eighteenth century, Marian Hannah Winter has concluded:

Although few would be prepared to acknowledge it, America, prior to the Revolution, was a dance-conscious country, and, after the Declaration, theatrical dancing had a vital relation to social and patriotic sentiment. . . . The American theater followed the London custom of combining spoken drama, music, and dancing, giving the public a well-rounded entertainment.[2]

She notes a dance enthusiasm so great in Charleston in 1786 that an audience rioted in protest when the dances they expected to see were not performed.

According to Winter, the dance entertainments that were popular in the eighteenth century were the harlequinade—a serious representation of a story from Ovid or "some other fabulous writer" interrupted by comic representations of the courtship of Harlequin and Columbine; narrative ballets based on popular ballads or derived from operas; rural ballets based on the national dances of Scotland and Ireland; nautical a.id patriotic pantomimes; and pantomime ballets based on popular novels and farces. Incorporated into these productions were country dances, character dances, court dances, acrobatic dances, tightrope dancing, ballet dances, and national dances.

Where did all the dances come from? Our dance traditions, like other aspects of our culture, derived from European models and were mainly under the direction of Europeans until well into the twentieth century. Ann Barzel has collected information about the migration of European dancers and teachers to America that began even before independence. Some of these were visitors; others settled here to perform, teach, choreograph, and organize companies. Before independence the dancers and dance masters were English. The first large influx of European dance personnel after independence came from France. As Lillian Moore has pointed out,

The French Revolution indirectly stimulated the development of American music, painting, dance, and theater. Many artists of outstanding talent were forced to flee France because of their intimate association with the aristocracy, and a great number of them found refuge in the United States.[3]

Barzel notes that "the French dominated the stage and the academies of the early 1800s, but the English supplemented" their work. By the second half of the nineteenth century there were also Italian, Hungarian, Swiss, German, and Danish dancers, choreographers, and teachers active in America.[4] Theatrical dance was an international art whose practitioners moved freely from country to country.

The first "serious" ballet presentation in America was *La Forêt Noire*, opening in Philadelphia in 1794 and starring a French dancer, Madame Gardie, and the first well-known American dancer, John Durang. It was in the 1790s—with the influx of French refugees—that the more lofty art of ballet appeared as distinct from other kinds of theatrical dance which were considered popular entertainment. The line is of course hard to draw. The popular entertainments included dancing that was called ballet, while productions such as *La Forêt Noire* featured specialty numbers and character dances, including a hornpipe.

In Europe, ballet had emerged as a court entertainment during the Renaissance. The first attempt to define and systematize the art came in the late seventeenth century, when Louis XIV of France established his Royal Academy of Dance and later added a dance school to his Royal Academy of Music. From that time, ballet developed as a professional rather than amateur activity, its technique becoming ever more difficult and exacting. The first professional female dancers appeared on stage in 1681, and from then on women became increasingly important as performers although men continued in positions of authority as teachers, choreographers, and theorists.

Public performances of ballet gradually began to supplant the traditional court performances in France and were popular among the aristocracy and the growing nonaristocratic rich. In 1713 a new professional ballet school was added to the Paris Opera and began to produce outstanding dancers who subsequently won acclaim all over Europe. Soon there were royal opera houses and theaters with ballet companies and schools in Italy, Austria, Russia, England, and Scandinavia.

By the middle of the eighteenth century the initial impetus had died down, and ballet became stereotyped. Later in that century, reform brought with it a great period of development that lasted well into the nineteenth century. Jean George Noverre and other reformers all over Europe developed the *ballet d'action* in which expression took precedence over virtuosity. In addition to demanding a closer relationship between movement and meaning, Noverre insisted on unification of choreography, plot, scenery, music, and costumes to create a dramatically cohesive theatrical dance form. Tales of shepherds and shepherdesses became a favorite theme, replacing stories from classical mythology. It was this phase of ballet that was brought to the newly established United States of America by French political refugees in the 1790s.

The reform begun by Noverre was interrupted by the French Revolution, but development continued in other countries, and eventually France resumed its prominent position. From about 1830 to 1850, during its Romantic period, ballet enjoyed another great era of creativity and widespread public interest in Europe and America.

In all the arts, including ballet, Romanticism was characterized by a breaking of classical restraints and an emphasis on intuition, emotion, imagination, and personal expression. Fascinated at once by the exotic and the occult, the Romantic choreographers favored plots that combined foreign settings with supernatural fantasy. The recurring theme, as described by dance historian Ivor Guest, was "man's pursuit of the unattainable, the infinite, exemplified in the hopeless love of a mortal for a fairy being."[5] Concurrently the predominance of the ballerina reached its peak, and with few exceptions, male dancing became secondary.

French Romantic ballerinas began to visit America in some numbers in the 1820s. The peak of American enthusiasm for the Romantic ballet was reached in the 1840s—stimulated by a two-year visit of Fanny Elssler, one of the great ballerinas of the Romantic era. Elssler took the country by storm. In spite of denunciations from sober members of the clergy, the American public flocked to her concerts and showered her with adulation. Despite the middle-class prejudice against theatrical performers, Elssler was applauded by ex-President John Quincy Adams, received by President Martin Van Buren, and escorted by President Van Buren's son. When she was in Washington, the members of Congress canceled meetings in order to attend her performances.

By this time America was beginning to produce its own accomplished ballet dancers. Best known were Augusta Maywood, Mary Ann Lee, Julia Turnbull, and George Washington Smith—all practitioners of the Romantic ballet, trained in its style and performing its masterpieces. One of the four, Augusta Maywood, achieved an international reputation.

During the second half of the nineteenth century, ballet declined in Western Europe and America. Romanticism had passed its peak, and no replacement appeared to recharge the art and give it new direction and vigor. What ballet there was on the American stage was for the most part in spectacular extravaganzas of the popular theatre.

The dance highlight of these years was *The Black Crook*, which opened in New York in 1866 and enjoyed great popularity. According to Lincoln Kirstein, this production "ran 475 nights, a record in that time, made $600,000 for its producers, $60,000 for Barrow, the author [Charles M. Barras], and was continually revived throughout the century." The plot of *The Black Crook* was a clumsy adaptation of the Faust tale, so secondary to the spectacle that its weakness did not interfere with the show's success. The dancers, apparently all female, were advertised as a "great Parisienne Ballet Troupe." Designated according to the traditional ballet hierarchy, they consisted of two *"premier danseurs assolute,"* (sic) one first *"premier"* soloist, eight second *"premiers"* and soloists, and twenty *"coryphees."* These dancers were advertised as coming from Paris, London, Berlin, and Milan, and appearing in America for the first time. In addition there were "Fifty Auxiliary Ladies selected from the principal theaters of London and America." The show received great publicity both for its merits and for the reputed near-nudity of its dancers. According to Kirstein,

The Black Crook got all the breaks, enjoying denunciations by the *Police Gazette*, and many more respectable journals, but more importantly from the Reverend Charles B. Smyth, who hired the Cooper Institute and harangued three thousand people for a whole afternoon on the sins of the show.[6]

The Black Crook was a bridge between classical ballet, with its high art pretensions, and popular theatrical dancing, with its catering to the mass entertainment market. It was followed by extravaganzas such as *The White Fawn*, which opened in 1868 and included a fish dance, a vegetable dance, a ballet of fireflies, and a ballet to Beethoven's Pastoral Symphony. There were many such shows, and in addition there were burlesques and imitations of the most popular of these spectaculars.

The field of the ballet extravaganza received further impetus with the arrival of the Kiralfy family from Hungary in 1869. The whole family performed as dancers, and the two brothers, Imre and Bolossy, produced and choreographed during the remainder of the nineteenth century. In contrast to other spectaculars with their white fawns, water lilies, nymphs of the rainbow, or sylphide queens (all drawn from the Romantic ballet), the Kiralfy brothers composed ballets on Jules Verne stories, the triumph of electricity, the fall of Rome, and Christopher Columbus.

Both the earlier Romantic ballerinas and the later ballet extravaganzas toured extensively throughout America and brought a good number of Americans into contact with theatrical dancing from one side of the footlights or the other. For these productions, only the stars and principal dancers were sent on tour. Chorus dancers and supernumeraries were hired locally and given as much as six to eight weeks of training by the ballet master, who traveled ahead of the main company. For elaborate shows as many as two or three hundred local people might be engaged. Many of these were factory girls who had come from the farms to work in the cities and whose families were too far away to know what they were up to. While the quality of this dancing must have been laughable at times, the numbers of people who performed or watched was probably significant for the development of a dance consciousness in America.

From the mid-nineteenth century on, ballet training became increasingly available in the cities, especially in New York. According to Barzel, numerous foreign dancers who came to America for professional engagements and tours had decided to stay and earn their livings by teaching. The most famous of these was Marie Bonfanti, Italian star of the first production of *The Black Crook* in 1866. She taught in New York until her death in 1913 and numbered both Isadora Duncan and Ruth St. Denis among her pupils.

The dancers trained in this period had several options if they decided to make a career of dance. They could perform in ballet spectaculars; they could work as dancer-actresses for one of the great theatrical producers, as both St. Denis and Duncan did; or they could present dance acts on the variety or vaudeville stage. Occasionally there was an opportunity for something more serious, like the productions of *Coppelia* and *Sylvia* presented by the short-lived American Opera Company in the 1880s.

But on the whole, ballet as a high art was not much in evidence from the days of Elssler until 1910, when the Russian dancers Anna Pavlova and Mikhail Mordkin were said to have electrified a Metropolitan Opera House audience in their first appearance in this country. And by then a new approach to dance as an art form was well under way: Duncan and St. Denis were already established artists outside the ballet tradition. The apparent scarcity of serious ballet in late nineteenth century America, however, may be deceiving. There were no performers as outstanding as Elssler or Pavlova, but there was probably a lively interest in the art if one is to judge by the number of teachers working and the popularity of ballet in the spectaculars.

That theatrical dancing has a history in America is clear. But what was its relationship with the country's life and culture? The most obvious point—noted by many writers—is that our theatrical dance in the eighteenth and nineteenth centuries was a European and not at all an American art. That is to say, American dance received its impetus, its goals, its standards, its style, its performers, and its teachers from Europe. We had not yet developed anything on our own that was strong enough to sustain the art independently or to contribute on an equal basis to the European tradition.

America did produce an increasing number of dancers, but their teachers were European and their model was strictly European. Mary Ann Lee, for example, "the first American dancer to attain nationwide fame as an exponent of the classic ballet," received her initial training from a former member of the Paris Opera Ballet who had settled in Philadelphia. In 1840, when Fanny Elssler made her American debut, Lee (at age seventeen) learned all of Elssler's character dances from the great ballerina's partner. Four years later, although already an established dancer with extensive American tours behind her, Lee went to spend a year at the Paris Opera Ballet School to improved her technique.[7]

Lee was typical in being an American performer of French ballet. Her aim was to come as close to its ideals and standards as she could—not to discover, seek, or promote other ideals or goals. The American public must have agreed that Europe should provide the model: Advertising that dancers were European was considered necessary in those days to attract an audience. Nor did anyone argue that America should develop its own, unique dance art. "High class" theatrical dance was European ballet. No other dance art existed or could be imagined. It is noteworthy that our political culture has impressed the world since the birth of the republic, and that within a few decades we began to develop an international reputation in literature. Yet throughout the nineteenth century we were slavishly adhering to a foreign dance art that concerned itself with naiads, sylphides, wilis, and other imported specters.

Theatrical dance was foreign to a large part of America in yet another way—as a career or activity it was outside the bounds of respectability. American theatrical dancers were probably without exception the children of theater people, the urban poor, or farmers. They were a subculture within the working class. Consider, for example, three of the leading ballet dancers of the midcentury. Augusta Maywood's parents were both in the theater. When they were divorced, her mother married a theater manager. Mary Ann Lee's father, a minor actor and circus performer, died early, and Lee began her stage career as a child to support herself and her widowed mother. And George Washington Smith was a stonecutter before he became a dancer.

In comparison, the three best-known American dancers of the 1930s were Martha Graham, Doris Humphrey, and Charles Weidman, who came from respectable middle-class families. The dance historian Olga Maynard has written that many chorus dancers of the nineteenth century worked in factories or as waitresses on the side. They had to, because a dancer's pay was so low. She says they were socially ostracized because they had the worst of reputations. One wonders who bothered to ostracize them; they were probably not the types to move in polite society even if they had not been dancers.

Considered from the other side, ballet never seriously engaged the cultural, social, political, or moral leaders of America before the twentieth century. They might have attended performances and enjoyed them immensely, but as far as we now know they did not subsidize the art with public or private funds. They did not argue its virtues and potential benefits for the nation. They did not marry dancers. And they certainly did not encourage their sons and daughters to become ballet dancers.

Dance was in a never-never land. It was beautiful, entertaining, popular—perhaps for the very reason that it offered a respite from everyday cares. One went to the ballet to watch beautiful women dancing in fairy tales and perhaps to forget the burning issues of the day. Later in the century, one attended the spectaculars to watch hundreds of beautiful women dancing in fairy tales, with all kinds of special effects added.

This is not to criticize ballet for being an escapist art form. As such, it was a source of pleasure and entertainment—and thus filled a social need. But why was dance not considered important in American culture until the development of the modern dance and the later emergence of a truly American ballet in the twentieth century?

The reasons, as we have seen, are complex. Ballet was under the control of Europeans and Americans who had neither knowledge of nor interest in American middle-class ideals and aspirations. Besides being committed to the European ballet model and its ideals and standards, ballet people were not close enough to the deepest American concerns to draw on them for direction and inspiration. On the other side, American leaders did not respect ballet or its practitioners sufficiently to expect anything from them, to support them, or to care whether we ever had a national dance art. Theatrical dance society and the great mass of American society were different cultures. America did not infuse the art with its particular idealism or esthetic vision, and ballet remained true to its European model (insofar as it could do so without the financial and institutional support that it enjoyed in Europe).

What dance needed to become a part of American culture, and what it finally gained in the twentieth century, can be better understood by comparing our dance history with the history of art (mainly painting) during the same period.

In *The Artist in American Society*, Neil Harris analyses American attitudes toward art before 1860, focusing on painting, sculpture, and architecture. Harris attributes the dearth of visual arts in colonial America to a similar lack in England in the sixteenth and seventeenth centuries, when the colonists left England. He points out that in neither America nor England was there a focused hostility to the arts themselves. Instead, there was ignorance about the arts, indifference to them, and antagonism toward those who supported them—and thus a resulting inhospitality. When interest began to develop during the eighteenth century, it was stimulated by the art of continental Europe.

In the course of the eighteenth century, as British painting developed, British artists and art theorists embraced and promoted a grander theory of the value of art than had been current in England up to that time. Influenced by continental art theory and practice, they argued that art had a "vast moral function, far greater than the task of entertaining for a day." As Harris explains it, "The artist's job was to outline the great truths which lay hidden in nature, to express the ideal, objective beauty inherent in all natural forms, and thereby to make virtue attractive and vice repellent."[8] The artist must be a philosopher rather than a mere craftsman.

Unhappy with their own lowly status as craftsmen and the low prestige of art, American artists developed similar ambitions. In the second half of the eighteenth century a few painters, notably John Singleton Copley, Benjamin West, and Charles Willson Peale, argued for the potential nobility and grandeur of art—characteristics un-known in American art up to that time. Such artists became "attached to the heroic ideals of high art, to the painting of history and great allegorical lessons." The Revolution and the establishment of the new nation gave great impetus as well as fresh and appealing content to these ambitions.

This idealistic approach enhanced art's prestige to some extent in America, but such aspirations—and their validity—were accepted by only a minority of artists and art enthusiasts in the early years of the Republic. More widespread was a suspicion of art and a condemna-tion of art as unworthy and potentially harmful to America's social and political goals. Many American intellectuals and leaders believed in "direct connections between the character of a people and the nature of its society" (a prominent theme in Western political theory). They felt that only a people "characterized by habits which are virtu-ous, pious, and restrained could maintain popular institutions and preserve a popular government as the creature and not the master of the national interest." They feared luxury, corruption, and depraved "manners, morals, and taste," seeing in these qualities threats to the success and stability of the great American experiment. Art elicited their suspicion on many counts. It cost money, yet it fulfilled no real need. Art was foreign and had aristocratic associations. Great art had been the product of only mature societies, prior to their downfall. Finally, art was sensual, and much of art's content was unsatisfactory on moral grounds.

American artists had to wait until the middle of the nineteenth century for their first widespread acceptance as an integral and so-cially acceptable part of the American scene. They attained this posi-tion largely through the efforts of the liberal clergy, who had adopted permissive attitudes toward the arts and entertainment. These minis-ters did not simply soften their former disapproval of the arts. They came to the belief that at its best, art was a moral activity; that ministers were really artists; and that artists were the equivalent of ministers. According to Harris, they began

propagating art ideas, urging aesthetic improvement, and proclaiming the artist's American mission. . . . Artists were admitted to full equality in the vast benevolent alliance forged to improve the nation's manners and morals. The great Civil War itself seemed only to intensify the need for the spiritual balm of art. Artists echoed clerical hopes, and meant their work to support idealistic objectives.[9]

Artists began to see their mission as essentially religious. They felt that only men of purity could be great artists. By means of this development, as Harris points out, "on a spiritual level, art had been legitimized to an extent incomprehensible to the Revolutionary generation."

The history of theatrical dance in America demonstrates a similarly inhospitable situation, if not more so. Americans could object to theatrical dance for the same reasons that made them suspicious of art. Ballet was conspicuously lavish and expensive, besides being an entertainment that could be traced to the decadent courts of Europe. It fulfilled no Christian or republican need. It was certainly sensual, and its content, as well as the reputation of its practitioners, seemed often unsatisfactory on moral ground.

In contrast to American art, which embraced idealistic values before the end of the eighteenth century, American theatrical dance had to wait for Isadora Duncan and Ruth St. Denis early in the twentieth century. Until they arrived on the scene there was no one to infuse dance with grandeur of vision and noblility of purpose. There was no sense of social mission coming from Europe, for the Europeans were more concerned with the internal developments of their art than with its relationship to society. The ballet community in America was too dependent on Europeans and too remote from mainstream American society to do anything on its own. And while the liberal clergy was becoming sufficiently broad-minded to approve of entertainment and to ally itself with art, it did not include ballet in its definition of art.

The process of legitimizing theatrical dance for America included many of the same steps that Harris has described in the process of art acceptance. The evils of dance had to be neutralized, grandiose goals had to be established and promoted, and dance had to be brought in line with some part of American culture. Dance had to develop positive values for American society, as we shall see.

We may still ask why the new American dance did not develop through the existing art dance—ballet. After all, the analogous development in art had stayed within the acceptable European painting tradition. We must remember, however, that more than half a century separated the two developments. By the time Duncan and St. Denis were growing up, an anti-traditional spirit was asserting itself throughout the Western world. The American social historian Morton White has characterized this as a revolt against formalism.

In his study of the phenomenon in the social sciences, White found that the anti-traditionalists shared certain characteristics: "They are all suspicious of approaches which are excessively formal; they all protest their anxiety to come to grips with reality, their attachment to the moving and vital in social life."[10] In the late nineteenth and early twentieth centuries, the revolt against formalism and the concurrent reexamination of basic premises was not limited to the social sciences or to America. Throughout the West, a vanguard of painters, sculptors, writers, musicians, and theatrical artists were just as suspicious of formalism and just as eager to find and to base their work on what was—or seemed to be—real.

In the late nineteenth century, ballet was still a strictly traditional art—and furthermore a decadent traditional art. To those who were seeking a freer dance expression, ballet seemed totally lacking in any potential for change and totally bereft of any elements consistent with the new values and goals. Ballet was excessively formal; it was out of touch with reality in its adherence to fantasy and an outmoded romanticism; and—perhaps most important—it had an unsavory reputation. As a consequence, dance innovators found their initial inspiration elsewhere—in a movement whose concern was not with dance per se, but with human expression in general.

NOTES TO CHAPTER 1

1. *The Cultural Life of the American Colonies, 1607-1763*, p. 178.
2. "American Theatrical Dancing from 1750 to 1800," p. 58.
3. "The Duport Mystery," p. 5.
4. "European Dance Teachers in the United States," pp. 62-70.
5. *The Romantic Ballet in Paris*, p. 3.
6. *Book of the Dance*, p. 346.
7. Lillian Moore, "Mary Ann Lee: First American Giselle," pp. 60-61, 65-66.
8. *The Artist in American Society*, p. 11.
9. Ibid., p. 300.
10. *Social Thought in America: The Revolt Against Formalism*, p. 6.

Above left: François Delsarte, ca. 1869. (From Percy Mackaye, *Epoch*, Vol. I.) Above right: James Steele Mackaye at about age 27. (From Percy Mackaye, *Epoch*, Vol. I.) Below: Portrait of Genevieve Stebbins from *Werner's Magazine* December 1895. (Theatre Collection, The New York Public Library at Lincoln Center.)

Above: "Achilles Robbed of Briseis," an example of Delsartian statue-posing. Below: "Grief," a Delsartian tableau. (From Elsie M. Wilbor, *Delsarte Recitation Book.*)

CHAPTER 2

The Genteel Transition: American Delsartism

In American theatrical arts, the movement against formalism and a concurrent development toward respectability received their earliest impetus from the nineteenth century field of study called *expression.* The forerunner of expression had been elocution, a system of voice and speech training that gained increasing importance in American education from the 1820s onward. From the mid-century, instructors in elocution emphasized gesture and physical motion more and more. The term "expression" came to include physical culture, pantomime, dramatics, and interpersonal communication as well as professional training for public speaking. Training in the narrower field of elocution had originally been an important part of education for men—especially for clergymen, lawyers, public readers, and lecturers. As educational opportunities for women expanded, training in expression came to be considered as useful and appropriate for young ladies and society matrons as for educated men.

Expression was taught by various methods, but the best known and ultimately the broadest in application was associated with the name of François Delsarte (1811-1871). This French music and drama teacher had spent many years in studying the movements, gestures, facial expressions, and vocal behavior of people in all kinds of situations to develop what he hoped was a complete, scientifically based system of dramatic expression. Underlying his technical system was an elaborate and mystical science of esthetics deriving from his personal interpretation of the Christian Trinity.

In America the original Delsarte system was expanded upon. Emphasis was placed on the esthetic theory and on physical culture and pantomime techniques that American Delsartians added to, or derived from, Delsarte's work. Because of these emphases, American Delsartism could be a more important influence on the development of an alternative dance art than any of the other schools of expression.

There were three phases of American Delsartism. The first began in the early 1870s and was closely associated with the professional training of speakers and actors. The second phase, coming to the fore in the 1880s, emphasized physical culture for the general public. It became particularly popular among women. In the third and broadest phase, which began in the late 1880s, Delsartian esthetic theory was elaborated and applied to all aspects of life.

The first phase of American Delsartism began with the only known American student of Delsarte, the well-known actor, dramatist, director, and theater inventor, Steele Mackaye (1842-1894). Mackaye worked with Delsarte in Paris from October 1869 to July 1870. He did not come to Delsarte as an unsophisticated beginner—he had been developing his own approaches to expression, pantomime, gymnastics, and esthetics for almost a decade. Delsarte soon discovered that Mackaye had something to offer that could complement and enhance his own work, so he invited the new pupil to teach with him. Thus Mackaye was not only a student of Delsarte but also to some extent a colleague.

The outbreak of the Franco-Prussian War forced Mackaye to return to the United States. Soon after his arrival, he was contacted by two noted Bostonians who had heard glowing reports of the collaboration of Delsarte and Mackaye in Paris. These were Lewis B. Monroe, founder and director of the Boston University School of Oratory, and Reverend William R. Alger, Unitarian clergyman and biographer of the American actor Edwin Forrest. Monroe and Alger encouraged Mackaye in his plans to lecture on the Delsarte system and to try to raise money to help Delsarte, who was in unfortunate circumstances because of the war. The three of them also hoped to bring Delsarte to America to lecture and teach in comfort and safety—a plan that was cut short by Delsarte's death in the summer of 1871.

The interest of the three friends in the Delsarte system did not wane after the death of the master. Mackaye continued to lecture and give lessons in addition to pursuing his career in the theater. He was most active in his promotion of the Delsarte system during the 1870s. In 1877 he established a school of expression in New York City, and the following year he gave an important series of lectures at Monroe's

School of Oratory. Monroe studied with Mackaye, then taught the system himself and included it in the curriculum of his school. Alger studied briefly with Mackaye and then spent a year (1871-1872) working under Gustave Delsarte, François's son, who taught in Paris after his father's death. After Alger returned he taught, wrote, and lectured on the system.

Of the first three American Delsartians, Mackaye was the only one to make a substantive contribution to the system as it was known and practiced in this country. How much of the system was Mackaye's has been open to question, since neither he nor Delsarte ever wrote a definitive treatise on the subject. The only literary remains of Delsarte—the beginnings of a book, one essay, and some random notes—deal with the theoretical principles of the system and how he arrived at them. For the rest, there are published works and unpublished notes by students of each of the men. From these writings—as well as on the authority of Mackaye's biographer and son, Percy Mackaye—it appears that, during its first ten years or so, the American Delsarte system consisted of theory from Delsarte and practical training procedures, called harmonic gymnastics, from Mackaye. The gymnastics were not just physical conditioning exercises, but rather, "exercises invented to develop equilibrium—flexibility—precision—and the gamuts of expression."[1] They formed a complete system of training which based techniques of emotional expression on a new or rediscovered esthetic of the human body. Fundamental to the whole method were principles of relaxation and naturalness, and these principles remained throughout the three phases. In the words of a later Delsartian, the training was designed

to give symmetrical physical development, and to take out the angles and discords, to reduce the body to a natural, passive state, and from that point to train it to move in harmony with nature's laws. The movements are without nervous tension, and all feats and exertions are discouraged.[2]

The harmonic gymnastics were designed for the training of actors and public speakers. Yet inherent in such an approach to expressive movement was a potential alternative to traditional ballet.

Whether or not Mackaye can be credited with inventing harmonic gymnastics has been confused by the fact that he minimized his own role in the development of the Delsarte system until his later years. As he grew older and saw Delsartism turn into a broad, popular, and sometimes faddish movement, he decided to speak out and claim credit for what he saw as basically his own system of expression. In 1892, he wrote:

In relation to Harmonic—or, as I first called them, Aesthetic Gymnastics,—they are, in philosophy as well as in form, absolutely my own alone, though founded, in *part*, upon some of the principles formulated by Delsarte.—*In the beginning of my teaching I never dreamed of separating my work from his,* for it was done in the same spirit as his, and I cared not for the letter, nor the fame.—It is only now, when others are teaching so much nonsense in his name, and basing it upon the truths stolen from me, that I am forced to do this.[3]

Mackaye's claim that he rather than Delsarte invented harmonic gymnastics was supported by Mme. Géraldy, Delsarte's daughter, who insisted that her father had *never* taught them. If we accept that the harmonic gymnastics were indeed Mackaye's, and that they were the basis of the total training system of American Delsartism, then we must conclude that what came to be known as the Delsarte system might have been more accurately named the Delsarte–Mackaye system.

Monroe and Alger did not add anything of their own to the Delsarte system, but each in his way contributed to its implantation into American culture. Until his death in 1879, Monroe was an enthusiastic advocate of the system. As a leader in the field of oratory, and as a teacher of subsequent leaders, he insured its prominence in his profession. Alger was active in teaching and lecturing from the 1870s until his death in 1905. He was particularly attracted to the mystical side of Delsarte's philosophy, and he alone of the first three American Delsartians popularized that aspect. Alger claimed that the Delsarte system was actually religious culture. He considered harmonic gymnastics to be "the basis of a new religious education, destined to perfect the children of men, abolish deformity, sickness, and crime, and redeem the earth."[4] Underlying such statements was the belief that man's physical nature was the manifestation of his spiritual nature rather than its antithesis, and this belief became popular as the Delsarte movement grew. Alger gave Delsartism a quasi-religious emphasis that justified attention to the human body as an expressive instrument. This emphasis remained with it and helped make possible—and morally acceptable—experimentation that would eventually lead to a new dance art. Alger's contribution is analogous to that of the liberal clergy who championed painting in the earlier period.

The representative figure of the second phase of American Delsartism, in which physical culture of the general public was emphasized, was Genevieve Stebbins. Beginning her career as an actress, Stebbins eventually became one of the most prominent popularizers of the

Delsarte system in America. It was she who carried the system far-
thest in the direction of dance.

Stebbins's elaboration of the Delsarte system derived from a
number of sources. It was founded on theoretical and practical material she had learned from Mackaye (with whom she studied from 1876
to 1878), from the Abbé Delaumosne (one of Delsarte's French students who had written on the system and whom she met in Paris),
and from unpublished manuscripts of Delsarte himself. In the preface
of one of her books she also acknowledged her debt to other teachers
in various fields of study. These included Regnier, a leading French
actor and professor at the Conservatoire in Paris, for lessons on
"dynamic nerve energy in the voice"; Dr. George H. Taylor for
"instruction upon the therapeutic value of different forms of exercise"; Dr. J. H. Buchanan for studies in anthropology; and Dr. Dudley
A. Sargent of Harvard gymnasium for various approaches to gymnastic exercises.[5] Elsewhere she mentioned having studied breathing
techniques with a "Hindu pundit" in London.

Stebbins furthered the Delsarte system in America through extensive work as teacher, writer, and performer. Most of her teaching was
in fashionable seminaries and academies for young ladies—and was
apparently sought equally by Protestant, Catholic, and nonsectarian
schools. In addition, she taught the Delsarte system and yoga
breathing exercises to such adult groups as a philosophy class and a
class of middle-aged women studying "nerve-gymnastics" (techniques for relieving nervous tension though correct breathing and
exercise).

Stebbins publicized the system through numerous books. Her
major treatise was *The Delsarte System of Expression,* which went
through six editions from 1885 to 1902. Other works included *Society
Gymnastics and Voice Culture* (1888), a shortened form of *The Delsarte
System of Expression; Dynamic Breathing and Harmonic Gymnastics—A
Complete System of Psychical, Aesthetic and Physical Culture* (1893),
which she described as "a complete outline of our teachings, and the
real principles, both metaphysical and vital, upon which they are
based"; and *The Genevieve Stebbins System of Physical Training,* which
was a manual of exercise and drills geared mainly for teachers of
physical education.

In the texts and titles of her works, Stebbins demonstrated an
ambivalence as to what she was actually presenting: the Delsarte
system or something of her own devising. She quoted heavily from
Delsarte in her books, identified her major work and fullest explication of what she taught as the "Delsarte System of Expression," and

gave Mackaye credit once in a while. But in other ways she tended to minimize the influence of both men—especially Mackaye—throughout her writings. Her strongest statement on this matter appeared in *Dynamic Breathing:*

This system of aesthetic gymnastics, originally suggested in a few brief hints by Mr. Steele MacKaye, was completely elaborated and carried out to the full perfection which it now enjoys by the present writer. She was the first to introduce the study of statue-poses and spiral motion into the fashionable schools of New York, and still more conspicuously to the public in her popular matinees at the Madison Square Theatre. . . . It was not to the principles of Delsarte, or to the *supposed instructions* of Mr. MacKaye, that she was able to evolve such an ideal system of culture; but to the principles set forth in this work, which have been the common property of the ages, known only, however, to a few who have devoted their lives to mystic and antiquarian research. [6]

In Stebbins's fullest explication of her version of the system, the sixth edition of *The Delsarte System of Expression,* she wrote that she had devised a training program based on Delsartian esthetic gymnastics, the Swedish Ling gymnastics, and yoga breathing techniques. She had combined these, she said, into a "perfect system of gymnastics which would bring into active use each of the three great principles of François Delsarte . . . *sequence, opposition, and correspondence* . . . all the elements essential to evolve beauty of form, graceful motion, and artistic presentation."[7]

While Stebbins added to the system and gave it her own special emphases, her theory and her system of classifying elements of expression rely heavily on Delsarte—deriving either from his own writings or from Delaumosne's book. Her practical system owes a great deal to Mackaye, since everything is based on relaxation (or decomposing, as it was often called) and poise (equilibrium), two of Mackaye's major concepts. In addition, her exercises for various parts of the body and her "gamuts of expression" (series of formulas for expressing any given emotion) derived at least in part from Mackaye.

To stress Stebbins's debt to her predecessors is not to imply that her own contributions were negligible. On the contrary, they were substantial and impressive. As a complement to relaxation techniques, Stebbins developed "energizing" techniques. These were exercises in which one set of muscles would be contracted while keeping the rest of the body relaxed. The idea was to control tension and effort—to use the body's energy efficiently rather than haphazardly.

Stebbins stressed the importance of correct breathing and taught breathing techniques. She developed the concept of human motion

patterning itself on what she considered the basic motion in nature—
the spiral curve, or spiral wave-motion (what we might call a spiral
successional movement). In the service of these concepts, as well as of
those she had inherited from Delsarte and Mackaye, Stebbins collected and created a multitude of exercises. What is most impressive
is that, if the nineteenth-century esthetic is stripped away, much of
her theory and many of her exercises conform to present-day approaches to dance and actor training.

Stebbins also increased the potential of the American Delsarte
system as a precursor of a new dance art in other ways. She differ-
entiated her work from the disesteemed ballet tradition and identified
what she taught with the kinds of expressive movement she felt
existed in the sacred dance of the Orient and the art of ancient Greece.
She thus directed attention to sources that would inspire the first two
artists of the new dance—Ruth St. Denis and Isadora Duncan. Asso-
ciating the new dance with remote cultures of the past and of the
mysterious East gave to dance a high tone and a sense of serious
purpose as well as providing a metaphysical and philosophical rationale for dance as an art. Furthermore, it reinvigorated the theory
and practice of dance by introducing new or rediscovered formal and
thematic ideas.

Stebbins also helped initiate the new dance by further developing
and publicly performing two Delsartian forms of expression: statue-
posing and pantomime. Elsie Wilbor, an ardent admirer of Stebbins,
described how, in a performance of statue-posing, her attitudes
"melt into one another, as the views of a stereopticon dissolve and
reappear before your eyes."[8] More important were Stebbins's pantomimic interpretations of a story, idea, or poem. There had of course
been pantomime in theatre from its beginnings. But the pantomime
of Stebbins and her followers was different: It was based on Delsarte's
laws of expression, Mackaye's harmonic gymnastics, and Stebbins's
own discoveries—what could by the 1880s be called the Delsarte–
Mackaye–Stebbins system of expression. Furthermore, Stebbins
added steps and rhythm to it, thus bringing it squarely within the
realm of dance as defined in that day. Ruth St. Denis saw Stebbins
perform both statue-posing and pantomime in 1892.

The curtain rose on a dark greenish background . . . and there stood an
exquisite woman in a costume made of soft ivory-white material that fell in
gracious lines to her feet, her figure beautifully proportioned, her blond head
proud and shapely. The strong light pouring upon her made her gleam like a
pearl against the dark setting.

  She moved in a series of plastiques which were based upon her understanding of the laws of motion discovered by Delsarte. Her poses were derived from Greek statuary and encompassed everything from the tragedy of Niobe to the joyousness of Terpsichore. Later she did a dance called the *Dance of Day*. At the opening of the scene she was lying on the floor asleep, and then, awakened by the morning sun, she rose with a lovely childlike movement to her knees and bathed herself in its rays. A light rhythmic step signified the morning and the noontide; and then began the slower movements of the afternoon, presently mingled with sadness as the late rays brought her slowly to her knees and again into her reclining posture of sleep.[9]

The progression from birth, through life, to death was to become a favorite theme in the new dance.

In her ideals, in her approach to movement as an expressive art, and in her performances, Stebbins introduced much of what would be credited by future generations to the invention of Isadora Duncan. Stebbins's achievement has been ignored by dance historians partly because she never acquired the notoriety during her lifetime that Duncan enjoyed, and partly because she performed infrequently, and then only in drawing rooms or at occasional ladies' matinees. Furthermore, no matter how stirring her performances may have seemed to Wilbor and St. Denis, they were probably far less brilliant than those of Isadora.

The whole tone of Stebbins's life was different. She was a sober, intellectual, middle-class teacher rather than a flamboyant, mercurial artist. Her aims were not to create the revolutionary new dance and new woman, but simply to teach and preach physical culture and esthetics to middle- and upper-class women, educating them to appreciate bodily motion as a healthful and pleasurable part of life. She provided them with evidence that an art based on physical expression could be high-minded and free from cheap sexual overtones—which was essential for middle-class involvement.

The third phase of American Delsartism was the broadest of all. Its ideal was to treat life as art and to enhance it according to the principles of Delsartian esthetics. This phase is best represented by Henrietta Russell, who had studied the principles with Gustave Delsarte in Paris, and by Edmund Russell, her husband, who had probably learned them from his wife.

From *A Delsartean Scrap-book*, a compilation of articles and clippings published in 1890, one would think that the Russells were the only noteworthy Delsartians around. They were featured prominently in the volume as the "high priest and priestess of Delsarte" who were giving lectures on "art study and criticism, color and house decoration, dress, grace, gesture and expression in oratory, acting, painting, and sculpture.''[10] Their range of interests was typical of the third phase and is reflected in the contents of the *Scrap-book* itself. It is also significant that the preface for the *Scrap-book* was written by a figure as prominent as Walter Crane, described as

a close associate of William Morris . . . second only to him in the development of the Arts and Crafts movement in England, and . . . also a very popular figure in the American cultural circles of his time. He [was known] variously as an illustrator of children's books, painter of classical and allegorical scenes, decorator, director of the Manchester School of Art, poet, and lecturer on art and socialism.[11]

Crane represents the artistic and social milieu in which Henrietta and Edmund Russell flourished. They shared with their friends in the arts and crafts movement a desire to bring beauty and harmony into all aspects of life—even the most trivial. The Russells moved gracefully amid the wealthy and socially prominent in London as well as at home. By means of lessons, lectures, and example, they taught everything from the appreciation of high art to the most attractive way of bowing or wearing a hat.

The Russells wrote no treatises on their version of the Delsarte system, so we have no authoritative statement of what they taught as physical culture. There are at least two descriptions of lessons, however. An account of Henrietta's teaching was written in 1891, when her instruction was the rage in high society. The occasion was a series of classes for the bluebloods of the Newport social set—the women of the prominent Astor, Vanderbilt, Whitney, and Stuyvesant Fish families and their friends.

The choicest cullings from the smart set meet twice a week to writhe, wriggle, bend and sway; to relax and decompose. . . . These pupils form spiral curves and make corkscrews of themselves, and at the end of each lecture fifty fair Four Hundred floppers fall at the feet of their fair instructor. For not only does Mrs. Russell teach these ladies how to bow, smile, walk and sit down, but how to fall gracefully and lie, a limp little mass of tangled lace and drapery, upon the floor. . . . Mrs. Russell puts her class through first, the relaxing motions, consisting of shaking fingers, rolling the head and hips, then the opposition of movement to get balance and poise, then the succession of movements during which the arms make one motion while the hips are doing quite another.[12]

In another report a young woman describes a private lesson she had from Edmund. She could afford only one meeting—it cost ten dollars—so she asked him to tell her as much as possible in the short time. He criticized her posture and carriage, her breathing, and her clothing (because it restricted her movement). What he suggested was a "course in falling" to take the stiffness out of her joints.[13] The Russells' physical culture sounds like diluted Stebbins adapted for the wealthy dilettante.

While Edmund Russell ceased to be prominent in American Delsartism after a few years, Henrietta was recognized as a major propagator of the system throughout her life. She appears in *Who's Who in America* from its first volume in 1899 until 1940, more than twenty years after her death. The *Who's Who* of 1899 records that she was the leading "Delsartean and chiefly responsible for the wide spread of Delsarte theories in this country; teacher of acting and Delsartean theory of art."

Ted Shawn reports that she was active as a Delsartian teacher and lecturer for the last thirty-five years of her life—until she died in 1917. He studied with her during her last years and brought her to Denishawn to lecture for his students there. He writes that she "further developed the movement which is closer to dancing than the system of Dalcroze. She experimented with Delsartian expression and was an inspiring teacher."[14] Henrietta apparently had much to offer the professional as well the dilettante. She is the only prominent Delsartian known to have had a direct influence on the innovators of the new dance.

A corollary to the Delsarte movement in both its second and third phase was the promotion of clothing reform. Less restrictive clothing—particularly for women—was recommended by the Delsartians initially for freedom of movement and better health. Stebbins had written:

Deep breathing is the first thing. Corsets must be consigned to the limbo of a superstitious age. It is useless to say that habit demands their continuance,—it is a false idea. They must be supplanted by lightly-boned waists, which do not cramp any part of the body.[15]

The Russells emphasized clothing reform far more—and for esthetic as well as health reasons. By example and argument they campaigned for this cause, hoping to overthrow men's fashions as well as women's. Edmund Russell once told an interviewer:

Men's clothes are a rank stupidity. They don't fit. They aren't graceful. They destroy health and all individual expression. . . . Your tailor makes your coat tight across the chest and tells you it is a good fit. But it is just too tight to admit of the fullest inspiration. The result is the chest is compressed down upon the abdomen. What is the result in the expressions of the ordinary attitudes? They become commonplace, vulgar.[16]

Style in movement is intimately linked with style in clothing. The Delsartian ideals of full respiration and fluid movement necessitated clothing different from what was fashionable in the late nineteenth century. And less restrictive apparel permitted and encouraged even more freedom of movement than the original reformers had ever imagined.

This third phase of American Delsartism was the last surge of the movement as a general cultural phenomenon. By the 1890s its creative energy was spent, and it became as mechanical and dogmatic as any rigid tradition. The Delsarte movement was over by 1900, but the best of Delsartian principles and innovations fed into the new dance movement and provided it with a foundation of ideas and techniques that it would draw on for at least a quarter of a century.

American Delsartism was not an esoteric cult for the few. There is ample evidence that it was known and taught throughout the country and touched a large portion of the middle and upper classes. It had something to offer those who had some education; there is no evidence that Delsartism made any inroads among workers or farmers. In a survey of the literature of elocution in *Werner's Directory of Elocutionists, Readers, Lecturers and other Public Instructors and Entertainers* (1887), F. Towsend Southwick, a teacher of pantomime and vocal expression, wrote: "By far the most important contribution to the art of expression which has yet been given to the world, is the method of François Delsarte, of which, thanks to his enthusiastic pupil, Steele Mackaye, far more is known in America than in Europe."[17]

The leaders of the movement—Mackaye, Stebbins, Henrietta Russell, and to a lesser extent Alger, Monroe, and Edmund Russell—taught, lectured, and, in the case of Stebbins, wrote extensively. Their students and followers, in their turn, spread the movement in ever widening circles through their teaching and writing.

The first extension of the Delsarte system in America took place when it was taken up by schools of speech training. Monroe introduced it into the Boston University School of Oratory in the 1870s. From there it spread to important private schools of speech such as the National School of Elocution and Oratory in Philadelphia; the Emerson College of Oratory in Boston; the Columbia School of Oratory, Physical Culture, and Dramatic Art in Chicago; the School of Expression in Boston; and the Leland Powers School of the Spoken Word in Boston. In these five schools, which were among the most important and influential of their kind, physical training was based on the Delsarte system.

The Delsarte system soon spread across the country. Out of fifty-eight American schools and teachers of expression, oratory, physical culture, dramatics, pantomime, and elocution that advertised in the back of *Werner's Directory* in 1887, sixteen offered the Delsarte System. Five of the others may be assumed to have incorporated Delsartian principles into their instruction, since the teachers had written books on that system or had studied at one of the speech schools. Of these twenty-one schools or teachers, six were in New York City, three in Chicago, and two in Philadelphia. There was one each in Boston; Denver; San Francisco; San Diego; Indianapolis; Logansport, Indiana; Lynchburg, Virginia; Concord, New Hampshire; and Providence, Rhode Island. One school gave no location. No other system was specified by name in any of the advertisements.

The Delsarte system was taught in other contexts as well. It was one of the three most prominent systems, along with German and Swedish (Ling) gymnastics, to be discussed and used in the burgeoning physical education movement of the 1880s and 1890s. William G. Anderson, an important leader of this movement, promoted "Americanized Delsarte" by offering it, under the direction of Emily Bishop, in the Chautauqua School of Physical Education which he founded in 1886 and directed until 1904. During Anderson's tenure the school trained an estimated 1200 to 1500 physical education teachers from all parts of the United States. In at least three colleges for women (Elmira, Rockford, and Smith), the Delsarte system was taught in physical education or elocution departments. And all this was in addition to the teaching of Stebbins, the Russells, and others in private academies and in privately organized classes for adults.

There is further evidence of the widespread diffusion of Delsartism in the number of books and articles about it that were published during its heyday. In the *Delsartean Scrap-book* of 1890, articles were compiled from a broad range of sources including the *Phrenological Journal;* a United States government publication; the *Northwestern Journal of Education; Voice Magazine; Scribner's Magazine; Harper's Bazaar;* and newspapers from Chicago, New York, Detroit, and Pittsburgh. Countless other articles were not included in the *Scrap-book.* And finally, between 1882 and 1902, at least twenty-one books were published in the United States on one or another aspect of Delsartism—and many of these came out in several editions. There is no question that, in the last decades of the nineteenth century, expression was a popular and respected field of study in America, and that the Delsarte system, with its emphasis on physical culture, was the best known and the most widely dispersed approach to expression.

The American Delsarte movement consisted of conflicting elements. From the beginning, in the work of Delsarte there was an inherent conflict. His was a true revolt against formalism—he searched for the "real" by studying living persons to see how they actually expressed themselves. But in his attempt to codify the elements of expression in an artificial triune system, he simply replaced one kind of formalism with another. When Delsarte used and taught his own system, it was probably not inflexible, but uncreative disciples are notoriously dogmatic, and some Delsartians on both sides of the Atlantic fell into that category.

Mackaye and Stebbins, on the other hand, felt free to use Delsarte's work as a stimulus to create a more useful and flexible training system based in part on his general philosophy and in part on other elements in their backgrounds. In their innovations in the realm of physical culture and expression, these Americans carried forward Delsarte's original revolt against formalism. The American Delsarte system developed new principles of movement based on relaxation, controlled and limited tension, easy balance, and natural flow of breath. It emphasized new or rediscovered design in movement: the spiral curve, successional movement, and the variety of movements suggested in classical Greek art. And in order to train students in the new principles and techniques, the American Delsartians compiled and created a body of exercises that could be used both for general physical culture and as a basis for further innovations in the art of movement.

Outside the realm of professional speech and theater training, American Delsartism was almost totally a women's movement. Nearly all the teachers, students, and authors were women, and Delsartism did much to liberate them from Victorian strictures. The Delsartians equated art with religion, the physical with the spiritual; and, bypassing the disesteemed ballet, they identified their expressive arts with the glories of ancient Greece and the mystical East. They thus provided a rationale for women to engage in physical activity and expression as well as offering a respectable, practical, and relatively easy form of physical training. The Delsartians furthered the cause of less restrictive clothing as a corollary to promoting greater physical freedom. Delsartian statue-posing and pantomime—the ultimate in refinement and gentility—became the opening wedge for the entrance of respectable women into the field of theatrical dance. Delsartism made it possible for two middle-class women not only to become professional dancers, but to initiate and lead a far-reaching renaissance of the art. Isadora Duncan and Ruth St. Denis began as Delsartians, but took that system of expression to such heights that it moved from the salon and the ladies' matinee to the grandest and most prestigious theaters and concert halls in Europe and America.

Since the heyday of the Romantic ballet the performers of theatrical dance have been mainly women, while the choreography and direction has been controlled by men. But it was women who led the way as innovators and choreographers as well as performers in the modern dance movement: Stebbins, Duncan, and St. Denis preceded Shawn; Doris Humphrey and Martha Graham preceded Charles Weidman. We might have had to wait much longer for the development of an alternative to ballet if women's freedom of choice and behavior had not expanded considerably as the nineteenth century came to a close. And Delsartism contributed significantly to that expansion.

NOTES TO CHAPTER 2

1. Percy Mackaye, *Epoch: The Life of Steele Mackaye*, I, 231.
2. Frederic Sanburn, comp., *A Delsartean Scrap-book*, p. 6.
3. Mackaye, *Epoch*, II, 270.
4. Shaver, "Steele Mackaye and the Delsartean Tradition," p. 212.
5. Stebbins, *Dynamic Breathing and Harmonic Gymnastics*, p. vi.
6. Ibid., p. 58, n.
7. *Delsarte System*, 6th ed., p. 401.
8. Ibid., addendum, pp. 485-486.
9. *An Unfinished Life*, pp. 16-17.
10. Edith Sessions Tupper in *Delsartean Scrap-book*, p. 107.
11. David Howard Dickason, *The Daring Young Men: The Story of the American Pre-Raphaelites*, p. 182.
12. Peggy Pendennis, "A Craze for Delsarte," p. 15.
13. *Delsartean Scrap-book*, pp. 91-100.
14. Ted Shawn with Gray Poole, *One Thousand and One Night Stands*, pp. 62-63.
15. *Delsarte System*, p. 412.
16. *Delsartean Scrap-book*, p. 103.
17. *Werner's Directory*, p. 249.

Above: Isadora Duncan reading in her garden.

Left: Theresa, Anna, Lisa, and Margot Duncan in a pose from one of Schubert's waltzes performed at l'Hotel des Artistes. Photograph by Apeda, New York, 1917. (Dance Collection, The New York Public Library at Lincoln Center.)

Isadora Duncan and Sergei Essenin in Germany before 1922 journey to the United States. (Dance Collection, The New York Public Library at Lincoln Center.)

CHAPTER 3

Passionate Revolt:
Isadora Duncan

As we have seen, American Delsartism helped to break down traditional attitudes toward our bodies, the way we move them, and the
way we clothe them. It touched many members of the middle and
upper classes of society with modern ideas and with actual physical
training.

But the American Delsarte movement was scarcely dance art or, in
its popular manifestation, theatrical art. For the most part it was a
system of physical culture for the layman. Its performance forms—
statue-posing, pantomime, and recitation—were strictly amateur. It
lacked a great artist to crystallize it into something more profound
and exciting than what was performed for society at-homes and
ladies' matinees. Then, near the turn of the century, Isadora Duncan
emerged as the first fullfillment of the Delsarte esthetic in dance form.
In her life and art, the movement against formalism in dance found its
first great exponent.

Born in San Francisco in 1878, Duncan spent most of her adult life
in Europe, where she enjoyed her greatest success. She performed in
the United States only occasionally throughout her life: between 1895
and 1899, at the beginning of her career, and in short visits in 1908,
1911, 1915, 1916, 1917, and 1922. She died in 1927.

In America Duncan never achieved popular success to the degree
she had in Europe. In later years she was positively loathed by that
portion of the public that saw itself as staunchly protecting this
country from the Red Menace. And yet her influence on American life

and thought has been profound. By the 1920s imitators abounded on the stage. Her ideas about art, education, and women's freedom gained wide acceptance among progressive educators, Greenwich Village bohemians, and the artistic avant-garde. Scores of admirers in Europe and America were committed to the ideals she represented. She became a symbol for those who sought freedom in any area of life, because in her they saw the embodiment of their own aspirations. She profoundly influenced ballet and educational dance, and she established the foundation for modern dance.

Duncan's trail-blazing was so extraordinary that one wonders about her background. What prepared her for this pioneering effort? In the realm of dance or movement, there were three approaches available in Duncan's early years that could serve as models and stimulate her mind and imagination. The first was ballet. The second, theatrical dance, consisted of the dance and pantomime presented in theatrical productions such as variety shows and dramas. The third was American Delsartism.

There were other kinds of movement in America at the time, among them gymnastic dance and folk dance. But except for her grandmother's Irish jigs (which Duncan credits as her first influence) the Duncan family, as middle-class culture-seekers, probably would not have come into contact with them—or would have scorned them if they had.

As she developed her own ideas, Duncan came to reject ballet completely. In her autobiography of 1927, she writes that as a youngster she had been taken to a famous ballet teacher in San Francisco, but she found that form of dancing so ugly and unnatural that she abandoned its study after only three lessons. She herself does not mention further ballet training, but her biographer Allan Ross Macdougall mentions that she also studied ballet in London with Katti Lanner, a leading English dancer, and in New York with Marie Bonfanti, former ballerina of *The Black Crook*—all this prior to 1899. We may never know her real attitude toward ballet as a child and adolescent. If Macdougall is correct—if she did seek further ballet training after leaving San Francisco—her early aversion may not have been as great as she later remembered it to be.

Whatever good she may have found in her early ballet lessons, Duncan did not seek a career in ballet, and she was soon confirmed in her distaste for that art. In "The Dance of the Future," an essay written in 1902 or 1903, she had this to say:

The school of the ballet of today, vainly striving against the natural laws of gravitation or the natural will of the individual, and working in discord in its form and movement with the form and movement of nature, produces a sterile movement which gives no birth to future movements, but dies as it is made.

The expression of the modern school of ballet, wherein each action is an end, and no movement, pose or rhythm is successive or can be made to evolve succeeding action, is an expression of degeneration, of living death. All the movements of our modern ballet school are sterile movements because they are unnatural; their purpose is to create the delusion that the law of gravitation does not exist for them.[1]

Duncan rails against ballet throughout her autobiography, at one point exclaiming, "I am an enemy of the Ballet, which I consider a false and preposterous art, in fact outside the pale of all art."[2]

Duncan's loathing for ballet was perhaps more intense and personal than that of many of her contemporaries, but her feeling was by no means unique. Genevieve Stebbins had written in 1902 that dancing

is not now pantomimic because the ideas expressed in its motion have been forgotten. I mean, of course, the dance of today as used in civilized countries. A thing cannot be strictly called pantomime unless the artist or performer understands what he is trying to express. If he does not, all real expression is lost, and it becomes purely gymnastic exercise, *the worst form of which is the so-called French ballet dancing.*[3]

In the early years of the twentieth century, the same idea was also current among intellectuals and artists in Europe. They shared the feeling that classical ballet had become a hollow form. And it had—outside of Russia. In what can almost be called her campaign against the ballet—as in her fervent espousal of positive ideals—Duncan was only carrying to extremes, publicizing, and embodying ideas that were already accepted by cultural progressives of both Europe and America. She did not initiate these ideas; she built upon them, illustrated their validity, and lent her glamour and genius to their cause.

In her formative years, Duncan also had some experience of contemporary theatrical dance and pantomime. After leaving San Francisco with her mother in 1895, she worked a short time at the Masonic Temple Roof Garden, a vaudeville theater in Chicago, doing a "peppy" dance with "skirts and frills and kicks." The manager had allowed her to do her "Greek thing" as well as the peppy dance he had insisted on—and he and his audience were quite satisfied with the result. But Isadora was not, and she soon quit. She writes about it with lofty disdain. "I had enough of trying to amuse the public with something that was against my ideals. And that was the first and last time I ever did so."[4]

Duncan next worked for Augustin Daly, one of the leading producers of the day, performing in a pantomime play, as a dancing fairy
in *Midsummer Night's Dream*, and in other small dance and mime
roles. With Daly's company she performed in New York and on tour
in the United States and Great Britain, all between 1895 and 1897. But
she was just as dissatisfied with this kind of work, although she did it
again briefly in London in 1900. She wrote that pantomime is "neither
the art of the dancer nor that of the actor, but falls between the two in
hopeless sterility." And she discovered that she was "not at all
interested in fairies"—her aspiration being rather "to express the
feelings and emotions of humanity."[5]

To someone with the ambition and the pretentions to art that
Duncan possessed, stage dancing at the turn of the century was too
formal, too rigid, too unnatural, or too silly. She could admire
Elizabethan drama and be profoundly moved by fine acting. But the
dancing that was to be seen in theatrical productions was too insub-
stantial to be attractive. Furthermore, in serious theater there was no
future for a dancer beyond playing a succession of these small and
flimsy parts.

The third approach to movement current in the late nineteenth century, American Delsartism, had nothing to offend Duncan's ideals.
On the contrary, it had much to offer her—in theory as well as in practice. It had the necessary characteristics to point to a new, more dig-
nified, more substantial direction for dance.

Macdougall makes a strong case for Duncan's having had direct
contact with Delsartian ideas, whether through teachers or books or
public presentations. He mentions a book on Delsartism found in her
possession, a statement attributed to her in praise of Delsarte that
appeared in print, and the story that the first person she sought out
when she arrived in Paris was Delsarte—not knowing that he had
been dead for thirty years. Ted Shawn corroborates the existence of
her printed statement on Delsarte. In March 1898, in an article entitled "Emotional Expression," Duncan is quoted as having said:

Delsarte, the master of all principles of flexibility, and lightness of the body,
should receive universal thanks for the bonds he has removed from our
constrained members. His teachings, faithfully given, combined with the
usual instruction necessary to learning a dance, will give a result exception-
ally graceful and charming.[6]

Further argument is provided by the dance historian and critic John
Martin, who rightly maintains that Delsartism was permeating the
theater at the time when Duncan was entering it. He suggests that
Duncan joined Augustin Daly's company in the mid-1890s at "the

crest of the Delsarte wave." But Martin argues that by this time, Delsartism had

begun to be crystallized into an academic code, and as such could scarcely have made any definite appeal to so free and independent a person as Isadora was even in her teens. . . . It would be difficult, indeed, to picture two more antithetical approaches than those of the rapt, impetuous, dynamic, young American girl, and the meticulous, note-making, logical-minded French-man, but both were seeking in their characteristic ways the secret of move-ment that should be genuinely expressive.[7]

Here Martin makes the common mistake of attributing all that was American Delsartism to Delsarte himself. As we have seen, Mackaye added to Delsarte, and others added to Mackaye. Duncan would have known the work of Stebbins or Bishop or one of the other American Delsartians—not the work of Delsarte himself. The silly ex-cesses of Delsartism had reached their peak by the 1890s. Still, books on the subject, coming fresh from Delsarte teachers, gave voice to ideas that Duncan stood for throughout her life.

It takes little probing to find the parallels between Duncan's beliefs and those of the American Delsartians. She agreed completely with the two basic ideas that underlay Stebbin's work: that classical an-tiquity represents the ultimate in artistic achievement; and that by means of the physical, the divine may be reached. The first visit to Greece that Duncan describes in her autobiography is nothing less than an ecstatic search for artistic roots. Even though she was sad-dened at the end of this journey by the realization that she could never actually be like an ancient Greek—that she herself was a mod-ern, "after all, but a Scotch–Irish–American"—she looked on Greek antiquity as a golden age in the history of man and as the foremost example of art and truth. Duncan often argued that she was not trying to do "Greek dancing"; she clearly recognized that as not only impos-sible but undesirable as well. What she sought from the Greeks was more basic:

In my art I have not at all copied, as is believed, figures from Greek vases, friezes or paintings. I have learned from them how to study Nature, and when certain of my movements recall gestures seen on the works of art, it is only because they likewise are taken from the great natural source.[8]

In another place she said that she spent so much time studying Greek art works

in order to steep myself in the spirit underlying them, in order to discover the secret of the ecstasy in them, putting myself into touch with the feelings that their gestures symbolized. Thus, in taking my soul back to the mystic sources of their rapture, I have, on my own part, found again the secret of Beauty that resides in that Holy of Holies.[9]

Isadora is in complete accord with Stebbins in seeing the arts of classical Greece as the culmination of true art.

The second major premise—the correspondence between the physical and the spiritual—is also central in the life-work of Duncan. She asks us to imagine a dancer whose "body is simply the luminous manifestation of her soul; whose body dances in accordance with a music heard inwardly, in expression of something out of another, profounder world." She writes that with her students, she has most of all tried to "bring to them a consciousness of this power within themselves, of their relationship to the universal rhythm, to evoke from the ecstasy, the beauty of this realization."[10] She has a strong belief in the power of dance to bring understanding. "Many profound secrets of the outer and inner meanings of Nature and natural forces can be given to the child through the dance," she argues.[11] And as for herself, she describes her quest:

I spent long days and nights in the studio seeking that dance which might be the divine expression of the human spirit through the medium of the body's movement . . . I . . . sought the source of the spiritual expression to flow into the channels of the body filling it with vibrating light—the centrifugal force reflecting the spirit's vision.[12]

It was above all the spiritual that Duncan consciously sought by means of dance. This fact is often ignored because of the hedonism and notoriety of her life, and because we tend to think that interest in the spiritual must be metaphysical. Duncan sought the spiritual as it was rooted in the body, in the earth, in the now. Her kind of spirit was in the Romantic and Victorian modes. Her spiritual kin were the Delsartians, Walt Whitman, Nietzsche.

Both Duncan's identification with the Greek ideal and her spiritual quest had enormous importance for the history of dance, especially in America. In the arena of professional dance, these concepts brought substance in terms of art and justification in terms of morals. They added reinforcement to a revolution in morals that was going on in all spheres of American life. They added to what had already been accomplished by the Delsartians. They helped do for dance what had been done for painting in the nineteenth century. On the negative side, they sometimes allowed dance to fall into a trap of moral and artistic pomposity.

Duncan's affinity with American Delsartism was not limited to these basic premises; she agreed with them in particulars as well. Her role in clothing reform, for example, is well known. She herself discarded the restrictive clothing that was fashionable in her day. She performed without tights, shoes, corsets, or arm-coverings, wearing only flowing draperies or gauze tunics. At times she chose neoclassic draperies and sandals for streetwear. The uniform for her students consisted of tunic, sandals, and a hooded woolen cape. One of the pupils has written:

I distinctly recall the sense of freedom I experienced in those light and simple clothes, which were the distinctive Duncan uniform and which would henceforth set us apart from other people. Goodbye petticoats and cumbersome dresses with bothersome hooks and high-buttoned shoes. [13]

But this student also describes the scorn and mistreatment the children suffered whenever they left the school grounds for a walk in the Berlin streets. As with the Delsartians, Duncan opposed the current fashions both for esthetic reasons and because restrictive clothing impeded the human body's breathing, functioning, and movement.

As the Delsartians rejected purely mechanical exercises and sought to correlate movement with mental or emotional states, so did Duncan. She criticized Swedish gymnastics as "a false system of body culture, because it takes no account for the imagination, and thinks of the body as an object, instead of vital, kinetic energy." [14] Of ballet she said:

The whole tendency of this training seems to be to separate the gymnastic movements of the body completely from the mind. The mind, on the contrary, can only suffer in aloofness from this rigorous muscular discipline. This is just the opposite from all the theories on which I founded my school, by which the body becomes transparent and is a medium for the mind and spirit. [15]

In her own teaching she sought means to relate the movements and exercises of her pupils with forms in nature and in art. She believed that "a child should never be given a movement that would not at the same time be an expression of the soul." [16]

Whatever direct contact Duncan may have had with American Delsartism, her work must be viewed as initially a part of that movement. Her basic concepts were the same as those of the Delsartians. These included the belief that physical culture was a sublime and healthy activity; that the natural and free were better than the artificial and restrictive; that sources for the natural and the highest in art could best be found in classical culture; that through the quasi-scientific analysis of movement, new potentialities might be found or old ones rediscovered; that restrictive clothing was both unbeautiful and unhealthy; and that physical exercise should be related to the mind, spirit, and emotions.

Delsartism, however, was far too limited a stimulus to account for all that Duncan's life and art have come to mean in the history of dance, education, and the liberation of women. We must look to her extensive reading, her familiarity with art, and her many and intimate contacts with contemporary artists and intellectuals.

Duncan's autobiography can be seen either as the story of a remarkable education or as an example of ostentatious name-dropping. Isadora herself and Macdougall, her sympathetic and admiring biographer, would lead us to believe that the dancer was a tremendously well-educated and cultured woman. Others have doubted this, seeing in her merely a flighty, flabby-minded prima donna with pretentions to intellectual achievement and spiritual profundity. William Bolitho, for example, an admirer of Isadora as "adventurer," derides her efforts as student or thinker:

It may easily be likely that of all this miscellaneous reading, and jack-daw culture, very little more than a collection of charming miscomprehensions, untargeted enthusiasms, and a general habit of skimming remained. Perhaps also, when her ruling prejudices formed, a jealous dislike, actually of sound knowledge and hard study, and all that can be founded upon them. [17]

It would be foolish to argue that Isadora possessed an orderly, scholarly, or contemplative approach to learning. From all accounts, she read and studied compulsively, gulping down in great drafts whatever stirred her emotionally. But is that any reason to doubt the extent of her knowledge, her sincerity in seeking it, or its influence on her art? I think not. On the contrary, her continual emotional intoxication (stimulated either by the object of study or by the teacher, who was more often than not in love with her) may have made her the most apt of pupils—open, responsive, greedy for understanding.

The way she learned lends credence to her claims to knowledge and understanding—progressing as she did from one thing to another as it fascinated her, or as it fascinated a man who fascinated her. What is more, Macdougall puts forward the credible argument that she commanded the respect and attention (not merely the lust) of too many artists and intellectuals for her to have been an intellectual dabbler. Finally, it seems unlikely that her art can be accounted for except in relation to her involvement with the art and ideas of the past as well as of her own time. So, suspending doubt, let us see what kind of education Isadora had—if she and Macdougall are to be believed.

Isadora's liberal arts education began in her home when she was a child. At a very early age, she developed an insatiable curiosity and a voracious appetite for reading which apparently stayed with her throughout her life. Isadora's mother subscribed to the agnostic beliefs of Robert Ingersoll and exposed her children to his nonmystical common-sense precepts. She also provided the family with the staples of nineteenth century culture: classic literature, Shakespeare, Fitzgerald's translation of the *Rubaiyat*, and Romantic and Victorian English literature. And as an accomplished pianist and music teacher, she was well equipped to familiarize her children with that art.

The whole family had an enduring, almost fanatic devotion to art; it was their religion, their life. Consequently, when they went to Europe they spent considerable time in museums and libraries and, in Greece, at temple sites—seeing, reading, studying, educating themselves in the main currents of Western tradition.

But Isadora did not have to rely on self-education alone. Wherever she went, artists and writers were eager to share what they knew with the glamorous young dancer. Early in her visit to London in 1899 she was taken up by one of the cultural elites of that city. Charles Halle, painter and director of the New Gallery (which featured modern painting), introduced her to a circle of painters, musicians, writers, and scholars. Some of these were avid Philhellenes who reinforced her interest in classical Greece and served as her instructors. For example, the neoclassic painter Sir Lawrence Alma-Tadema accompanied her on tours of museums where Greek art was on view. She wrote later that Alma-Tadema had "pushed me towards the studies of the ancient Greek vases which permitted me to reconstruct the movements of the antique dance."

A young poet, Douglas Ainslie, read to her from Swinburne, Keats, Browning, Rossetti, Wilde, and William Morris. Halle himself educated her in the work of the pre-Raphaelites and of Whistler and Tennyson. He took her to see the great Ellen Terry in plays of Shakespeare, the 1900 Italian season of Eleanora Duse, and the Paris Exhibition of 1900 where she saw, among other things, the sculpture of Rodin and the performances of Loïe Fuller and the Japanese dancer Sada Yakko.

One of the most significant aspects of the English phase of Isadora's education was in the realm of music. In 1900 Charles Halle arranged to present her in three recitals at the New Gallery. In the first of these (March 16), as was her custom, she danced part of the program to passages from classical literature and part to music such as Mendelssohn's *Spring Song* and Ethelbert Nevin's *The Water Nymph*. It was then that John Fuller-Maitland, an eminent musicologist and critic, encouraged her to concentrate on dancing to music rather than literature, and "to good music, and specifically the waltzes of Chopin." Finding her receptive to his suggestion, he worked with her on the Chopin to help her "get the right elasticity of rhythm."

Two others must also be given credit for broadening her musical scope at this early stage. Sir Hubert Parry, a neoclassic composer, lectured on the relation of music to dance at her July 4 New Gallery program. Arnold Dolmetsch, well known for his research on early instruments and music, introduced her to early Italian music and directed the orchestral accompaniment for her "Dance Idyls from Fifteenth-Century Masters" program at the New Gallery on July 6. According to Macdougall, "the programme was so eruditely arranged that one suspects the knowledgeable overseeing of both the well-known artist [William Richmond, who opened it with a lecture on Botticelli and the Primavera] and the eminent musicologist."[18] Isadora's choice of music for dancing and her skill at integrating the dance with the music have long been considered two of her major contributions to dance—and this is apparently where it all started.

The English experience, coming when it did and with such intensity, had a profound effect on Isadora's subsequent development. It broadened her understanding of art and music and focused her interest on classical Greece as a source and inspiration. But as the dancer in her youth was always open to more learning, and as there were willing teachers wherever she went, her education did not stop there. In Paris, Charles Noufflard, Halle's nephew, "set out to complete my education in French art, telling me much about the Gothic, and making me appreciate for the first time the epochs of Louis XIII, XIV, XV, and XVI."[19]

Another friend, André Beaumier, a French writer, taught her a great deal about French literature. He read her Molière, Flaubert, Gautier, Maupassant, Maeterlinck's Pelléas et Mélisande.

Isadora relates that in Germany a young man named Karl Federn had come to her.

He decided it was his mission to reveal to me the genius of Nietzsche. Only by Nietzsche, he said, will you come to the full revelation of dancing expression as you seek it. He came each afternoon and read me "Zarathustra" in German, explaining to me all the words and phrases that I could not understand[20]

In Germany she was also learning the language and reading Schopenhauer, Ernst Haeckl, Kant. She spent the summer of 1904 at Bayreuth, studying Wagner. At the same time, Heinrich Thode, art historian and an ardent admirer, was reading to her from Dante as well as from his own works.

Duncan became well acquainted with Greek art, English painting, and works of the Italian Renaissance. She associated with and served as subject for many artists. She knew and used the music of such composers as Monteverdi, Gluck, Beethoven, Mendelssohn, Chopin, Liszt, Franck, Tchaikovsky, and Wagner, and among her friends and colleagues she counted musicians, composers, and musicologists. In the realm of theater she knew, saw the work of, and exchanged ideas with David Belasco, Mrs. Patrick Campbell, Gordon Craig, Eleanora Duse, Sacha Guitry, Henrik Ibsen, Henry Irving, Lugné-Pöe, Jean Mounet-Sully, Stanislavsky, and Ellen Terry. And of the contemporary dance world she saw and met Diaghilev, Nijinsky, Loie Fuller, Mathilde Kschesinskaya, Anna Pavlova, and Sada Yacco with her Japanese troupe.

Most of this education took place prior to 1904, when Isadora was twenty-six. More than twenty years later, she singled out a few great figures who had influenced her the most. After what she claims was an intensive siege of reading on the history of dance, theater, and Greek music at the library in Paris (probably 1900-1902), she said the only people who could be her dance masters were Jean Jacques Rousseau, Walt Whitman, and Nietzsche. Saying that her dance had its beginning in her grandmother's Irish jig, she continues:

I learned it from her, putting into it my own aspiration of Young America, and finally, my great spiritual realisation of life from the lines of Walt Whitman. And that is the origin of the Greek dance with which I have flooded the world.

That was the origin—the root—but afterwards, coming to Europe, I had three great Masters, the three great precursors of the Dance of our century— Beethoven, Nietzsche, and Wagner. Beethoven created the Dance in mighty rhythm, Wagner in sculptural form, Nietzsche in Spirit. Nietzsche was the first dancing Philosopher.[21]

How seriously to take this assertion that her art stemmed from the work of philosophers, poets, and composers is a question related to the assertions about her education. But the claim appears believable and the education real in the light of her art, her life, and her writings.

It must be borne in mind that Isadora used what she needed for inspiration or reinforcement and discarded the rest. She also considered Rousseau one of her most revered dance masters. The reason? She read in *Emile, or The Education of the Child* that "a child should not be taught to read or write until its twelfth year. Up to that time all of its knowledge should be gained through music and dancing." She considered this a great discourse on education. She certainly would have agreed also with Rousseau's belief in the goodness of nature and the evils of civilization. But what of his prescription for the education of the girl-child—that girls should be trained only in the arts of taking care of men? Isadora, the fervent crusader for women's freedom, ignored this, picking out the truth that was meaningful to her and apparently discarding the rest. But such practice does not mean she was any less committed to or sincere about the truths she chose.

Whitman, she maintained, was her first great inspiration. From his vision of America singing, she imagined "the mighty song that Walt heard, from the surge of the Pacific, over the plains, the voices rising of the vast Choral, of children, youths, men and women, singing Democracy." This in turn gave her "a Vision—the Vision of America dancing a dance that would be the worthy expression of the song Walt heard when he heard America singing."[22] But in this she looked forward rather than back. The forty-nine-year-old woman reminiscing in 1927 has grandiose visions of herself and her mission that can hardly reflect what was in the mind of the teenager before 1900.

Perhaps she did read Whitman in her youth, although it must have been daring to do so; but the youthful enthusiasm would have taken a form different from that of the Isadora of 1927. The mature woman had experienced more and had become somewhat socially conscious and politically aware. We may never know what Isadora thought and felt in her youth because we have only her own testimony, colored by the passage of time and the distortions of memory. But whether it was the younger or the more mature Isadora whose imagination was seized by Whitman, he had much to offer her.

Whitman glorified the body—its look, its movement, its uses. Near the beginning of "I sing the Body Electric," he asks, "And if the body were not the soul, What is the soul?" In this long ecstatic hymn of praise to men and women in their work, their love, their physical selves he says, "If anything is sacred, the human body is sacred."

> O I say these are not the parts and the poems of the
> body alone, but of the soul,
> O I say now these are the soul![23]

This is but another manifestation of the belief found in Delsartism that the physical and spiritual are one—that one reaches the "soul" only by means of the body. The soul or spirituality is not degraded; the body is exalted. What an ardent reader these lines must have found in Isadora!

The Delsartians apparently did not extend their quest for physical liberation to sexual freedom and the glorification of sex—or at least they did not write about it. But both Isadora and Whitman did—or at least they *did* write about it. In "A Woman Waits for Me," Whitman writes:

> Without shame the man I like knows and avows the
> deliciousness of his sex,
> Without shame the woman I like knows and avows hers.[24]

When might Isadora first have read these lines? As the innocent maid she describes herself to have been before her first love affair at age twenty-four? Or as the more experienced woman who had learned "that love might be a pastime as well as a tragedy—" a pastime to which she could give herself "with pagan innocence"?

Gone were the days of a glass of hot milk and Kant's "Critique of Pure Reason." Now it seemed to me more natural to sip champagne and have some charming person tell me how beautiful I was. The divine pagan body, the passionate lips, the clinging arms, the sweet refreshing sleep on the shoulder of some loved one—these were joys which seemed to me both innocent and delightful.[25]

Like Whitman, Duncan did not hide her fascination with sex, although concealment would have been the conventional thing for a woman of her day. Instead she exalted it, as he did, flaunting her love of it and her right to it.

Duncan shared—or emulated—the ecstatic quality of Whitman as early as 1902 or 1903 when she wrote "The Dance of the Future," a lecture she delivered in Berlin during her controversy with the defenders of ballet in that city. Most of the piece consists of rational argument, but at the close she builds to an emotional peak on the twin themes of the new dance and the new woman—the woman who "will dance not in the form of nymph, nor fairy, nor coquette, but in the form of woman in her greatest and purest expression," the woman who will "realize the mission of the woman's body and the holiness of all its parts."[26] Perhaps she was thinking of Whitman's lines:

> Welcome is every organ and attribute of me, and of
> any man hearty and clean
> Not an inch or a particle of an inch is vile, and
> none shall be less familiar than the rest.[27]

Duncan builds on this theme:

From all the parts of her body shall shine radiant Intelligence, bringing to the world the message of the thoughts and aspirations of thousands of women. She shall dance the freedom of women. . . . Do you not feel that she is near, that she is coming, this dancer of the future! . . . She will help womankind to a new knowledge of the possible strength and beauty of their bodies. . . . She will dance the body emerging again from centuries of civilized forgetfulness. . . . "Oh, do you not feel that she is near, do you not long for her coming as I do?" . . . Oh, she is coming, the dancer of the future: the free spirit, who will inhabit the body of the new woman; more glorious than any woman that has yet been; more beautiful than the Egyptian, than the Greek, the early Italian, than all the women of the past centuries—the highest intelligence in the freest body![28]

This was written when she was twenty-four or twenty-five, at the beginning of her concert career, before she had opened her first school.

In later years Duncan's ecstatic vision had a different content. But in that difference it paralleled yet another aspect of Whitman's vision—it ranged across the vast panorama of her abandoned America. When accused of being unfaithful to the land of her birth, she answered that she loved America, that she and her students were "the spiritual offspring of Walt Whitman." Her dance, she said, was not Greek. On the contrary, "It has sprung from America, it is the dance of the America of the future," its movements came from all the great regions of America. Perhaps her best-known effusion in this vein is this:

I see America dancing, beautiful, strong, with one foot poised on the highest point of the Rockies, her two hands stretched out from the Atlantic to the Pacific, her fine head tossed to the sky, her forehead shining with a crown of a million stars. . . . [American children of the future should] come forth with great strides, leaps and bounds, with lifted forehead and far-spread arms, dancing the language of our pioneers, the fortitude of our heroes, the justice, kindness, purity of our women, and through it all the inspired love and tenderness of our mothers.

When the American children dance in this way, it will make of them Beautiful Beings worthy of the name of Democracy.

That will be America dancing.[29]

Her vision was to be realized in the 1930s, albeit in dance styles she would have found harsh and ugly. And her passion for Whitman would be shared by dancers of that decade.

And what of Nietzsche? She felt gratitude toward this philosopher who had written: "I would believe only in a god who could dance," and "we should consider every day lost on which we have not danced at least once" She refers to these and other passages frequently in her writings. *Thus Spake Zarathustra,* apparently her favorite work, is liberally sprinkled with such direct statements in praise of dancing: "Only in the dance," says Zarathustra, "do I know how to tell the parable of the highest things." Zarathustra describes the intoxication of the dance:

At my foot, frantic to dance, you [O life] cast a glance, a laughing, questioning, melting rocking-glance: twice only you stirred your rattle with your small hands, and my foot was already rocking with dancing frenzy.

My heels twitched, then my toes harkened to understand you, and rose: for the dancer has his ear in his toes.

I leaped toward you, but you fled back from my leap, and the tongue of your fleeing, flying hair licked me in its sweep.

Away from you I leaped, and from your serpent's ire; and already you stood there, half turned, your eyes full of desire.[30]

This must have had a profound effect on Isadora. To such a culture-worshipper, a philosopher was like a god—and here was a great, respected philosopher describing the entanglement of the human with life in terms of a frantic, playful dance. No wonder she wrote that "the seduction of Nietzsche's philosophy ravished my being."

In addition to direct reference to dance, other thoughts in *Zarathustra* would stimulate Isadora and give weight and reinforcement to her ideas. Like Whitman, Nietzsche lauds the physical, the here and now, and the concrete as more real and meaningful than dead dogmas of God, wisdom, eternity. He writes of "a new pride my ego taught me":

no longer to bury one's head in the sand of heavenly things, but to bear it freely, an earthly head, which creates a meaning for the earth. . . . It was the sick and decaying who despised body and earth and invented the heavenly realm and the redemptive drops of blood.[31]

He says there is "more reason in your body than in your best wisdom," and later: "Alas, there has always been so much virtue that flew away. Lead back to the earth the virtue that flew away, as I do—back to the body, back to life, that it may give the earth a meaning, a human meaning."[32] One can imagine Isadora reading these lines as if they were written especially for her.

Finally, Nietzsche's mocking irreverence toward the things men took seriously, his criticisms of the pettiness of human life, and what has been called his Dionysian exuberance would attract Isadora. She could hardly have achieved a philosopher's understanding of Nietzsche. And she may have disregarded or rejected his sometimes unflattering depiction of women—or have considered them applicable only to traditional women. Nevertheless, *Zarathustra* probably furnished a vision of dance in relation to life more grandiose and all-inclusive than anything even Isadora had imagined up to that time. It also provided reinforcement from the respected realm of philosophy for her intuitive beliefs that truth resided in the body and on the earth, and that marriage is generally a "poverty of the soul in pair."

Perhaps most significantly, *Zarathustra* gave her the ideal of the *Uebermensch* to take as her own. Isadora never spoke of this concept from Nietzsche, but in her adoration of the great as well as in her own life as she and others have depicted it, the superior being is an ever present theme. Bolitho has pointed out that it is rare for a woman or a

rich man's son to accomplish something in the world—or to be a true
adventurer—because they have alternatives: marriage, in the case of
the woman. Could it not be that Nietzsche's philosophy encouraged
Duncan to strive for great ends, impractical though they often were?

Beethoven, Wagner, and other great composers contributed to
Isadora's art by giving her models to emulate as well as direct inspiration. The dancer sought to achieve emotional intensity and ecstasy
through movement, and it was their music that allowed her to do so.

Walter Damrosch raises his baton—I watch it, and at the first stroke there
surges within me the combined symphonic chord of all the instruments in
one. The mighty reverberation rushes over me and I become the Medium.
. . . Voluminous, vast swelling like sails in the wind, the movements of my
dance carry me onward—onward and upward, and I feel the presence of a
mighty power within me which listens to the music and then reaches out
through all my body, trying to find an outlet for this listening.[33]

In a less intoxicated vein she has written:

The great geniuses of music alone have had rhythm in their work. That is why
I have danced to the rhythms of Bach and Gluck, of Beethoven and of
Chopin, of Schubert and of Wagner, because practically they alone have
understood and expressed the rhythm of the human body.[34]

Why did she value Beethoven and Wagner above the other composers? First, it is likely that they simply moved her the most. Second,
she particularly admired what they did or attempted to do.

Wagner, she maintains, "re-found the drama." No matter that, in
her opinion, he mistook the role of the chorus by transferring it to the
characters. No matter that he tried to combine music and drama,
which at one time she believed to be impossible. No matter that it was
"an offense artistically to dance to such music." Still, Wagner was
"the closest approach to a musician for the dance." She had used his
music because it was capable of "awakening the dance that was dead,
awakening rhythm."

It must be remembered that until Duncan showed the world a
different path, dance had had the most superficial relation to its
music—and dance music itself was light and unsophisticated. This
was as true for ballet as for popular theatrical dance. So when Duncan
talks about the great music awakening the dance, or awakening the
rhythm, she is referring to the ability of this music to stir the dancer to
create an equivalent expression in dance—something that had not
been done before.

Beethoven meant just as much to Duncan as did Wagner. His music
was stirring, heroic. The Seventh Symphony and other works of his
had been composed upon specific dance rhythms, and throughout

her life, Duncan felt a deep gratitude to all the great figures, be they composers, philosophers, artists, whatever, who honored dance by writing about it, using its themes, or praising its virtues. Finally, it was the work of Beethoven—especially his Seventh and Ninth Symphonies—that gave Duncan the grand vision of her mature years: in place of the solo dancer, a "vast ensemble," an "orchestra of dancers . . . which would be to sight what the great symphonies were to sound."[35] Unfortunately, this was another of many visions she herself never realized.

So we glimpse the education of Isadora Duncan. Many questions remain—questions as to the effect on Isadora's art and thought of Eleanora Duse and other actors, the theories of Ernst Haeckl and Charles Darwin, the writings of Kant and Schopenhauer, Nietzsche's other writings, and the dance of Sada Yacco and her Japanese troupe, to mention only a few. And how much did she know of the works of Freud and Marx, figures she mentions in her writings but does not elaborate upon?

But even this cursory glance at her education gives some idea of its significance in her life and work. Without it, she could hardly have asked the questions and developed the goals that we find in her art and her writings. There was no precedence for this in dance. Compare her work and that of Loie Fuller, remembered as the "butterfly girl," a dancer who discovered a beautiful effect in the combination of swirling · draperies and imaginative lighting. Her innovations in lighting are her only claim to remembrance today. Loie Fuller did not have the breadth of vision to seek education and to use it that would have made her dance more than technical gimmickry.

In contrast to Loie Fuller and every other contemporary dancer, Duncan achieved breakthroughs not only in dance but in her lifestyle as well. In dance she provided an alternative to classical ballet, an art that even in its few brilliant manifestations was neither relevant nor exciting to a good portion of the cultured public in the first third of the twentieth century. She initiated the attack against formalism in dance, seeking first principles, trying to learn just what movement was, where it came from, and how it could be developed.

Duncan looked for answers not only in the works of thinkers, artists, and musicians. She also studied her own body and observed movement in nature. She describes how she tried to discover "the central spring of all movement, the crater of motor power, the unity from which all diversities of movement are born, the mirror of vision for the creation of the dance."[36] After concluding that the solar plexus was the source of movement she next sought

a first movement from which would be born a series of movements without

my volition, but as the unconscious reaction of the primary movement . . .
such as the first movement of fear followed by the natural reactions born of
the primary emotion, or Sorrow from which would flow a dance of lamenta-
tion.[37]

From nature and art, she realized that there was a relationship
between the mover and its movement—today we would say a relationship between form and function. She found classical statues
beautiful because "the movement of each was in direct correspondence with the form and symmetry of each."/She looked to
nature and found that the movement of any particular element was
"peculiar to its nature" and "eternal to its nature." Waves, for example, moved in their characteristic way; each animal had its own way;
the earth itself had a movement in harmony with its nature.

Duncan justified her approach to dance by drawing an analogy
between humans and animals:

The movement of the free animals and birds remains always in correspondence to their nature, the necessities and wants for that nature, and its
correspondence to the earth nature. It is only when you put free animals
under false restrictions that they lose the power of moving in harmony with
nature and adopt a movement expressive of the restrictions placed about
them.

So it has been with civilized man.[38]

She argues that man will have to return to nakedness "not to the
unconscious nakedness of the savage, but to the conscious and acknowledged nakedness of the mature man, whose body will be the
harmonious expression of his spiritual being."[39]

Duncan's mind was not sufficiently incisive to question what was
really natural in animals or in men. Did she mean to do away with
reading books, living in houses, eating cooked food? No. On one
hand Duncan preached the back-to-nature dogma as part of her battle
against the forms, artificialities, and restrictions that she disliked. On
the other, she used what she called nature as source material for ideas
and as justification for her dance, clothing, and sexual behavior. And
in the larger sense, Duncan's yearning for nature looked back to the
similar yearning of the earlier romantics and was contemporary with
the fear of man's dehumanization as victim of the mass technological
civilization he himself has created.

The questions Duncan asked were not new, but they were new to
dance. She was the first to compare dance to the other arts and set
them up as her model. And she was the first to try to find an organic
basis for the art. She then became the model that would be emulated
at least through the 1960s. To give some prominent examples: Be-

tween 1915 and 1920 Gertrude Colby, Margaret H'Doubler, and Bird Larson were seeking first principles of movement for educational dance. In the late 1920s Doris Humphrey, Charles Weidman, and Martha Graham were seeking to discover dance and specifically American dance. And as late as 1967 Anna Halprin, a leader of the avant-garde in American dance, said that what she was really searching for was "the genesis of movement." One may readily ask why the sources of dance have had to be rediscovered so often in the twentieth century, especially when no one worried about them before that. In part the answer may be that in America, the aftermath of Duncan and progressive education (in which dance has figured prominently) has been a continuing distrust of formal and technical rigidity. As forms of technique have hardened into dogma, there has always been a rebel to challenge their validity and offer something new.

Duncan was influential or at least prophetic in two other aspects of dance. The first is that of using dance for political or social statements. The Isadora who reflected post-romanticism often overshadows the Isadora who prefigured the revolutionary romanticism of the 1930s. Her technique and style were perhaps different, but the content and the intent of dances such as the *Marseillaise*, the *Marche Slav*, and the *Internationale* were the same as those of the fervent militants of America's "red decade": heroism, love of country (not necessarily one's own), and revolution. Two descriptions will suffice. A contemporary critic has described "her fiery miming of the *Marseillaise*":

In a robe of color of blood she stands enfolded; she sees the enemy advance; she feels the enemy as it grasps her by the throat; she kisses her flag; she tastes blood; she is all but crushed under the weight of the attack; and then she rises triumphant, with the terrible cry, *Aux armes, citoyens!* Part of her effect is gained by gesture, part by the massing of her body, but the greater part by facial expression. In the anguished appeal she does not make a sound, beyond that made by the orchestra, but the hideous din of a hundred raucous voices seems to ring in our ears.[40]

The performances of this dance—first in Paris and then in New York—before the United States entered World War I generated hysterical enthusiasm, according to this critic. The same critic has described her *Marche Slav* by Tchaikovsky as telling of the Russian moujik's rise from slavery to freedom.

With her hands bound behind her back, groping, stumbling, head bowed, knees bent, she struggles forward. . . . With furtive glances of extreme despair she peers above and ahead. When the strains of *God Save the Czar* are first heard . . . she falls to her knees and you see the peasant shuddering under the blows of the knout. The picture is a tragic one. . . . Finally comes the moment of release and here Isadora makes one of her great effects. She does not spread her arms apart with a wide gesture. She brings them forward slowly and we observe with horror that they have practically forgotten how to move at all. They are crushed, these hands, crushed and bleeding after their long serfdom; they are not hands at all but claws, broken, twisted, piteous claws! The expression of frightened, almost uncomprehending, joy with which Isadora concludes the march is another stroke of her vivid imaginative genius.[41]

This could be the description of any number of revolutionary dances in America during the thirties—with the exception that the later dancers *would* have spread their arms wide and would have tried to express undiluted joy at the end.

A second element in Duncan's work never went beyond the ideal for her. She writes in at least two places of a desire to break down the barrier between audience and performer. Not liking the custom she found in Moscow of a public that did not applaud, she wrote, "on the contrary, one should work toward a theatre in which the public would take part more and more in the performance, even in eventual responses, singing of the choruses, etc."[42] In a fuller statement she developed the idea:

I have always deplored the fact that I was forced to dance in a theatre where people paid for their seats; . . . where the spectators' attitude is that of people who sit still and look but do not participate. Of course, in moments of great enthusiasm when the audience arises and applauds, they manifest a degree of dance participation. But I have dreamed of a more complete dance expression on the part of the audience, at a theatre in the form of an amphitheatre where there would be no reason why, at certain times, the public should not arise and, by different gestures of dance, participate in my invocation. Something of this must have existed in the ancient cults of Apollo and Dionysus. Something of this still exists in the rituals of the Catholic Church and also in the Greek church, where the congregation alternately rises, kneels and bows, in response to the invocation of the priest.[43]

What a remarkable leap! Written in 1927, that vision is thirty or forty years ahead of its time. It was not until the end of the 1950s that happeners and event-makers began to merge the audience with the performers, and only during the 1960s have we seen the growth of a holy theater devoted to ritual—The Living Theater, Jerzy Grotowski's Polish Lab Theater, and the Bread and Puppet Theater of New York, for example.

Without a doubt, Isadora Duncan looked both backward and forward with her art and her life. Her work represents a watershed in the history of American dance, because she created something that became the foundation for a contemporary dance art. Equally beyond doubt is the fact that a contemporary dance art would have developed without her—after all, there were Ted Shawn, Ruth St. Denis, and their school, as well as the people working in educational dance. But it was the good fortune of the dance world that she did exist, for her vision had great scope and deep roots, and thus the foundation was that much stronger.

NOTES TO CHAPTER 3

1. *The Art of the Dance*, pp. 55-56.
2. *My Life*, p. 164.
3. *The Delsarte System of Expression*, p. 469. Italics mine.
4. *My Life*, p. 28.
5. Ibid., pp. 33, 36.
6. Ted Shawn, *Every Little Movement*, p. 82n.
7. *America Dancing*, p. 145.
8. *The Art of the Dance*, p. 102.
9. Ibid., pp. 139-140.
10. "The Dance in Relation to Tragedy," p. 757.
11. *The Art of the Dance*, p. 124.
12. *My Life*, p. 75.
13. "Follow Me: The Autobiography of Irma Duncan," p. 13.
14. *My Life*, p. 90.
15. Ibid., p. 165.
16. *The Art of the Dance*, p. 119.
17. *Twelve Against the Gods*, pp. 287-288.
18. *Isadora*, pp. 53-56.
19. *My Life*, p. 69.
20. Ibid., p. 141.
21. Ibid., pp. 340-341.
22. Ibid., pp. 339-340.
23. *Leaves of Grass*, pp. 98-105.
24. Ibid., p. 105.
25. *My Life*, p. 254.
26. *The Art of the Dance*, pp. 62-63.
27. "Song of Myself," in *Leaves of Grass*, p. 51.
28. *The Art of the Dance*, p. 63.
29. Ibid., pp. 49, 50.
30. Nietzsche, *Thus Spake Zarathustra*, p. 224.
31. Ibid., p. 32.
32. Ibid., p. 76.
33. Duncan, *My Life*, pp. 223-224.
34. Duncan, *The Art of the Dance*, p. 95.
35. Duncan, *My Life*, p. 213.
36. Ibid., p. 75.
37. Ibid., p. 77.

38. Duncan, *The Art of the Dance*, pp. 54-55.

39. Ibid., p. 55.

40. Carl Van Vechten, "The New Isadora," in Paul Magriel, ed., *Isadora Duncan*, pp. 30-31.

41. Ibid., p. 31.

42. Duncan, *The Art of the Dance*, p. 112.

43. Ibid., p. 123.

Opposite page: Ruth St. Denis in four poses from *Radha*, 1906. (From *The American Stage of Today*.

SIGHT

TASTE

MISS

RUTH

ST. DENIS

SMELL

TOUCH

55

Ruth St. Denis and Ted Shawn in 1918. (Dance Collection, The New York Public Library at Lincoln Center.)

CHAPTER 4

The American Way:
Ruth St. Denis and Ted Shawn

Isadora Duncan was the first great American pioneer of modern dance. Ruth St. Denis was the second. In many details the lives of the two women ran parallel. They are believed to have been born the same year—1878. Both were products of American Delsartism. Both studied ballet with Marie Bonfanti in New York. Both launched theatrical careers in the mid-1890s, and each worked for Augustin Daly, among others. Dissatisfied with such work, each abandoned it to create her own vision of a great dance art—Duncan in 1897; St. Denis in 1904. Both did extensive research in libraries and museums, gathering material upon which to base their art.

Both traveled to Europe, where they met some of the same important people. In 1900 both saw Loie Fuller and the Japanese dancer Sada Yacco at the Paris Exposition, and both were deeply impressed. They each elicited the admiration of many European artists and intellectuals. Rodin, for one, not only sketched them both, but tried—unsuccessfully—to seduce each of them. Both declared the intention never to marry, a vow they each eventually broke.

Both dancers received the first support for their independent work from society patrons. And it was in Germany that each enjoyed her greatest initial success. In that land, first Duncan and later St. Denis were taken up by a circle of sophisticated artists and intellectuals who took the art of the dance far more seriously than analogous groups did in other countries. The two dancers' wonder and delight at this response is recorded in their autobiographies. Both dancers demonstrated a strong sense of mission throughout their careers, and both founded schools to carry their work forward.

Despite the parallels in their lives, two more different women or dancers could hardly be imagined. With Nietzsche, Duncan sought to "lead back to the earth the virtue that flew away . . . back to the body, back to life, that it may give the earth a meaning, a human meaning."[1] In contrast, St. Denis wished to "become a rhythmic and impersonal instrument of spiritual revelation."[2] Duncan's autobiography is the story of a life lived fully in the moment; St. Denis's, the story of her spiritual quest and its victory over art and human love. Isadora's mind conceived a grand vision of America dancing—which she herself was unable to realize. St. Denis's vision concerned more than anything else her own spiritual development, and yet she—with Shawn—was largely responsible for the accelerated spread of dancing across America.

We have seen what fed Duncan's art. St. Denis's was nourished on a far different diet. As a youngster she eagerly grasped at any movement or dance training she was offered. At first there were lessons in Delsarte given by her mother out of a book. In New Haven, Connecticut, Mrs. Dennis had met a Delsartian teacher named Madame Poté, who said she had trained with one of Steele Mackaye's pupils. Madame Poté demonstrated the exercises for Mrs. Dennis and gave her a book to guide her in teaching them to her daughter.

In 1892, St. Denis saw Genevieve Stebbins perform, and later wrote, "at this early age nothing so beautiful had ever entered my life." In this recital, as we have seen, Stebbins performed both statue-posings and an interpretative dance called *The Dance of Day*. For the young and sensitive adolescent it was a revelation. "I glimpsed for the first time the individual possibilities of expression and the dignity and truth of the human body, moving in that Grecian atmosphere of grace and light."[3] Later, she attempted to create a dance in the same style—a classic dance in a Greek costume and done in bare feet.

St. Denis certainly valued the Delsartian contribution to dance. Around 1915, she and Shawn engaged Mrs. Hovey to give a series of lectures on Delsartism at Denishawn, from which she said she profited as much as the students. In an article published in 1924 she wrote that Delsarte had done the most to formulate the "laws of causation that govern movement." In 1927 she wrote a testimonial letter to Percy Mackaye in which she expressed her debt to the Delsarte teachings of his father. She said that she appreciated the Delsarte system because it gave the first theoretical basis for the new dance, and because it stressed the "law of correspondence between emotion and motion, thought and gesture, spirit and form."[4]

What St. Denis responded to in Delsartism was the pure theory as devised by Delsarte himself. The philosophical bases of American Delsartism were antithetical to her ideas and inclinations. The Delsartians found their most meaningful source in Greece; St. Denis found hers in the Orient. St. Denis courted the spiritual through the physical—through dance—but with yogic rather than humanistic aspirations. She sought ultimate escape from the physical into the realm of the spirit. As we have seen, while yoga found its way into American Delsartism, it was not really used to achieve release from physicality. It was simply an attractive and exotic method of physical culture.

In Duncan's writings and in her development as an artist we can trace a consistent link with the philosophical bases of American Delsartism. She accepted classical Greece as her most revered source; she manifested in her life as well as in her art a correspondence between the physical and spiritual that was rooted in the earth—in the here and now. She created an art of expression that carried the Delsartian ideal to a more sophisticated and less schematic level. But there was always an American Delsartian spine to Duncan's work— although, as she matured, she broadened her scope far beyond anything the Delsartians had imagined.

In contrast, St. Denis simply used the Delsarte system the way it was used by other contemporary theater people—as a technical means whereby gesture and movement could be "scientifically" derived. St. Denis's vision of art and her life were far more influenced by other sources.

Besides training in and exposure to Delsartism, the young St. Denis also took dancing lessons. When she was about ten years old her mother enrolled her in a class in Somerville, New Jersey. The instructor, Maude Davenport, was teaching social dance—a means of instilling manners and grace into children that has had a long history in the United States. There were boys and girls in the class, all dressed up to learn how "to grasp their little partners with a clammy hand and lead them to some other place on a huge, slippery floor."[5] St. Denis mentions the schottische, but aside from that she does not remember what she learned there. Miss Davenport, recognizing special ability in her pupil, sent her to New York to audition for the dancing master Karl Marwig. He was enough impressed to offer her free lessons, and in 1893 St. Denis and her mother managed to move to New York so as to take advantage of those lessons and launch Ruth's career on the stage.

All St. Denis writes about Marwig is that he was a "fashionable teacher and taught willowy debutantes how to conduct themselves on ballroom floors." On her first visit to his studio, she showed him a "little Spanish dance with a tambourine," which he criticized for its non-Spanish arm movements.

From somewhere—from Delsarte exercises, from Maude Davenport's or Karl Marwig's classes, or from her own resourcefulness—St. Denis learned to do kicks, cartwheels, backbends, and splits. These stunts were the stock in trade of the variety-show dancers of the 1890s, and this was the kind of thing she performed in her early engagements.

In the mid-1890s, St. Denis studied ballet with Marie Bonfanti. Another influential dance experience was seeing Loie Fuller and Sada Yacco perform in 1900 in Paris. She has written of this:

In America I had seen many imitations of Loie Fuller . . . so I was somewhat prepared for her astonishing and beautiful performance. . . . She had a heavy body and never a very polished technique, but she was an inventive genius and brought a wealth of richness to both the dance and the stage. A little of this I recognized that night, but my real excitement and wonder was stirred to an unbelievable pitch by the extraordinary acting of Mme. Sadi Yaco.

For the first time I beheld and understood the beautiful austerities of Japanese art. Here, in her dancing (she was, of course, both dancer and actress), was the antithesis of the flamboyant, overblown exuberance of our American acrobatics. Here was a costuming in which the colors were vivid, yet so related to the mood that they seemed to emanate from a different palette. Her performance haunted me for years, and filled my soul with such a longing for the subtle and elusive in art that it became my chief ambition as an artist. From her I first learned the difference between the words "astonishing" and "evoking."[6]

Delsarte lessons, dancing lessons, learning acrobatic tricks, all these had stimulated St. Denis's interest in dancing and had given her a knowledge of the scope of American dance in that day. Seeing Sada Yacco perform—like seeing Genevieve Stebbins years earlier—provided her with the knowledge that dance could be more than it usually was and with the inspiration to expand its boundaries herself.

Another important part of St. Denis's education was provided by her extensive theater experience. From 1893 to 1898 she performed whenever she could in vaudeville engagements. Then, until 1904 she worked more as an actress than as a dancer in the legitimate theater—first for Augustin Daly and later for David Belasco, two of the leading theatrical producers of the day. Thus she had eleven years on the professional stage before beginning her independent career.

St. Denis's delight in sumptuous and spectacular theatricalism was first evoked by a visit to the Barnum and Bailey circus before she was ten years old. On the second part of the program was the "colossal spectacle of *The Burning of Rome.*" It was there, she writes, that a passion for spectacles [was] lighted, and the spiritual descendants of *The Burning of Rome* pervaded my whole career. Nothing had ever been seen before like these houses going up in flames, with the Colosseum a black silhouette at one side. As a grand finale a ballet of a hundred angels floated about on the stage, dressed in costumes made of ribbons. I could scarcely contain my excitement. All the way home I sat in a corner of the carriage, my face tense and pale, and would not speak to anyone. The first thing I did when I got to the farm was to go into the garret and slash up a pair of Mother's old curtains to create my first dancing costume.[7]

A few years later, St. Denis was taken to see Imre Kiralfy's pageant ballet, *Egypt Through the Ages.*

Of course, it was a toe ballet and, viewed from the vantage point of today, the choreography and the costumes were totally unsuited to the theme of various episodes in the life of Egypt, but to me it contained such magic that for months afterwards I dreamed of it.[8]

Thus even before she began to work in the theater, she had developed a partiality for theatrical spectacle.

St. Denis's experience with David Belasco confirmed her attachment to spectacle and educated her in the mechanics of producing it. The dance historian Christena L. Schlundt writes that Belasco

had a predilection for the unusual, the intense, even the bizarre. He produced dramas not representative of familiar life, but rather chose incidents from the unusual, the colorful, the sensational. Then he set these incidents in meticulously realistic settings. This combination of the romantic with the realistic was the Belasco tradition. . . .[9]

St. Denis never turned her back on these early lessons in showmanship. When she finally realized what it was she wanted to do, "I suddenly discovered that all I had absorbed from D. B. [David Belasco] . . . was now to be turned into rich and wide channels."[10] And throughout her life, her productions incorporated every element of rich theatricalism that she could manage: lavish sets, elaborate costumes, supernumeraries to set the scene, and a sense of pace that would leave no one bored. This was later one of the major factors in the success of Denishawn productions on both the concert and the vaudeville stage.

Again, the contrast between Duncan and St. Denis is striking. Duncan had worked in theater, but only for a short while. Her independent ideas developed earlier than St. Denis's, and she sooner became dissatisfied with what the theater had to offer her. But Duncan rejected theatricalism along with the theater. She eschewed lavish sets, elaborate costumes, the trappings of show business. She performed in simple draperies before plain blue curtains and saw herself as a soloist rather than as part of a production. If Duncan had been willing to work in vaudeville and variety houses, she undoubtedly would have failed because of her austerity.

St. Denis's intellectual education also differed markedly from Isadora's. While St. Denis's father subscribed to the ideas of Robert Ingersoll and Thomas Paine, her mother, to whom she was much closer, was of a serious religious nature. Mrs. Dennis was trained as a doctor—a profession she had to give up because of her health—and her library consisted of books on religion and medicine. In this house there was apparently no classical literature, no Shakespeare, no Romantic and Victorian *belles lettres*, only an occasional novel. Ruth's reading consisted of the Bible, Emerson, Brother Lawrence's *The Practice of the Presence of God,* or *The Idyll of the White Lotus,* a romantic religious allegory by Mabel Collins. St. Denis writes that at the age of twelve she read Kant's *Critique of Pure Reason,* which started her on a "lifelong absorption in metaphysical literature." One wonders how, since she admits that she did not understand it at all. But throughout her life, St. Denis did indeed look for spiritual inspiration as insatiably as Isadora devoured culture.

The first landmark in St. Denis's spiritual quest was Christian Science. In 1903 at the age of twenty-five she read Mary Baker Eddy's *Science and Health with Key to the Scriptures.* This threw her, she writes, into a "condition of spiritual ecstasy" for some weeks and "left as a residue a love of spiritual things and a realization of metaphysical values" that stayed with her.[11]

The Christian Science philosophy that so enraptured the young St. Denis is at the opposite pole from the philosophy that excited Duncan. The latter, as exemplified in the writings of Whitman and Nietzsche, denies the existence of the spiritual apart from the physical. Mary Baker Eddy, in contrast, calls everything spirit and denies the existence of the physical altogether. In her view "the description of man as purely physical, or as both material and spiritual,—but in either case dependent upon his physical organization,—is the Pandora box, from which all ills have gone forth, especially despair."[12]

The American Delsartians, Duncan, and Duncan's mentors sought a cosmic harmony in the laws of physical nature. They considered traditional Christian dualism between the spirit or the mind and the body to be the height of disharmony. Eddy took the opposite position, finding disharmony in the "erring human mind [which] is inharmonious in itself," and from which "arises the inharmonious body." She warned against any attention to the body—against physical culture, exercise, diet, hygiene. She deemed it best to ignore the body completely.

Obviously, St. Denis did not follow this philosophy all the way.

Like Duncan, she used what was helpful to her and ignored the rest. What Christian Science gave her was an ideal, along with general goals she sought to realize through dance. St. Denis describes herself as victim of a conflict between the artist and the saint within her—a conflict that later became triune with the appearance of human love on the battleground of her soul. To outward appearances, the artist often dominated. But the artist was always shaped and channeled by her inclination to sainthood. As she put it, "the visible career as well as the subjective regions which gave rise to that career were all taking shape in these deeply conscious moments of my spiritual adolescence."[13]

With equal insight, she realized that her spiritual awakening could have been triggered by "any of the other scriptures of the world." But, as it happened, the Christian Science philosophy was the one that gave her the spiritual nourishment she was seeking and confirmed her in the belief, already latent, that the most important aspect of life for her would be the spiritual.

During the following theatrical season (1903-1904), while on tour again for Belasco, St. Denis underwent another ecstatic experience. In a drugstore she saw a poster advertising Egyptian Deities cigarettes. On it was a picture of

a modernized and most un-Egyptian figure of the goddess Isis. She was sitting on a throne, framed by a sort of pylon. At her feet were the waters of the Nile with lotus growing. Her knees were close together; her right hand was on her right thigh, while with the other hand she held a lotus-tipped staff.

She obtained the poster and spent days gazing at it, enraptured, for

here was an external image which stirred into instant consciousness all that latent capacity for wonder, that still and meditative love of beauty which lay at the deepest center of my spirit. In this figure before me was the symbol of the entire nation, culture, and destiny of Egypt . . . the figure, its repose, its suggestion of latent power and beauty, constituting to my sharply awakened sensitivity a strange symbol of the complete inner being of man. . . . It was, however, not merely a symbol of Egypt, but a universal symbol of all the elements of history and art which may be expressed through the human body.

This experience gave St. Denis a focus for her spiritual/artistic ambitions: She would create a dance art as grand in scope as the vision given her by the poster.

The poster must have brought back memories of Stebbins's "Myth of Isis" pantomime and of Kiralfy's *Egypt Through the Ages*, both of which she had seen as an adolescent. In any case, she decided to create an Egyptian ballet in which she would be Isis. The ballet would depict the

rise and fall of [Egypt's] destinies during the period of a day and a night. The day would show her emerging from the unknown, developing to her zenith at noon when her kings and her priests and her artists brought a nation to its prime, and then declining with alarums and wars and invasions to the time of her death. The night would be given to her concept of imortality and its processes of attainment.

St. Denis spent the next two years researching and planning the ballet that would manifest her spiritual vision. She visited museums and libraries; she talked to anyone who might know anything about her theme. Eventually she shifted the scene from Egypt to India, because she found greater spiritual stimulus in India. But she never forgot the "image of *Egypta* [that] had set into vibration an inward state that would inevitably express itself . . . and it made no difference what the artistic environment or race culture was that [she] transmitted through the dance."[14]

In the beginning of 1906, St. Denis launched her first East Indian ballet, *Radha*. During that spring she performed it on sixty-eight dates in New York and once in Washington. She then left for Europe, where she performed in variety theaters and opera houses from June 1906 until June 1909.

While in Europe, St. Denis studied yoga for a time. She said of it:

This complex and highly developed concentration upon the developments of the human personality in terms of spiritual and physical discipline had appealed to me strongly. As a dancer, intensely aware of the dominion which comes from the sense of bodily control, I was stirred to find that India had indeed given profound thought to this question.

This study led her to create another Indian dance, *Yogi*. She believed that this dance, more than any other, demonstrated her "inescapable necessity to manifest in outward form that state of consciousness which has attained a certain intensity of illumination."[15] Her interest in yoga was in part compatible with her inclinations toward Christian Science. Although yoga utilizes physical exercise—something Mrs. Eddy abhorred—its ultimate goal is consistent with the Christian Science goal of absolute freedom from the physical body and the material, finite world.

By the time St. Denis returned to the United States she had completed a suite of five East Indian dances. Besides *Radha* and *Yogi* it included *Incense, The Cobras,* and *Nautch*. She had enchanted Europe with her art and brought home with her a grand European reputation —a prerequisite to success in the United States. She was soon enjoying that success to the full.

With St. Denis, as with Duncan, the vision of a broad, significant new dance art came from outside Western theatrical dance. The experiences that inspired both dancers to break with the past were not available in either the dance or the theater of that day. Thus it was that Duncan could say that her dance masters were Whitman and Nietzsche, Beethoven and Wagner. And in this sense, St. Denis's first dance masters were Mary Baker Eddy and the Egyptian Deities cigarette poster. The performances of Stebbins, *The Burning of Rome, Egypt Through the Ages,* and Sada Yakko that St. Denis had seen in earlier years undoubtedly contributed to her art, but it was the cigarette poster in combination with Eddy's philosophy that motivated her to action. Christian Science opened her heart to the vast realm of the spirit and taught her to love that above all. The poster gave her a theme with which she could place art in the service of religion and thus satisfy two inclinations at once. Her vision was subsequently deepened and broadened by extensive research into the philosophy and culture of the Orient. Like Duncan, St. Denis neither sought nor achieved a scholar's understanding of her sources. She simply used what she needed in creating her unique and revolutionary dance art.

We must take notice of the superior potentiality of St. Denis's choice of dancing masters, in contrast to Duncan's, for the development of dance in America. At the beginning of her career, Duncan was as genteel as any Delsartian. But before long she took the Delsartian creed to its logical conclusion, aligning herself with a philosophy and a way of life distasteful to the majority of her countrymen.

With St. Denis, the opposite was true. Her background, inclinations, and aspirations kept her always close to middle-class American values and led her to two of nineteenth century America's favorite "religious excitements": Christian Science and yoga. These were a part of the New Thought movement, or the "Boston Craze," as described by Gilbert Seldes. The disciples of New Thought, according to Seldes, "agreed that sobriety and virtue, chastity and self-improvement were the foundations of a good life." Above all, they sought "harmony with the unbounded universe," and the merging of the finite into the infinite.[16] There was nothing in such a creed to alienate St. Denis from the American public. On the contrary, it embodied the most acceptable American middle-class ideals and values.

St. Denis's interest in the wisdom of the East also placed her in line with an American literary and philosophical tradition. Beginning with the transcendentalists and continuing on into the twentieth century, outstanding Americans have discovered in oriental thought spiritual truths compatible with their aspirations and personalities. Emerson and Thoreau were the first, but the orientalist interest in

America was not confined to men of such stature. By the Victorian era, works of Vedanta, Sufi, and Buddhist literature were available in popular as well as scholarly editions, and English and American poets were writing frequently on oriental themes. Among the most widely read poems of this age were Edward Fitzgerald's version of the *Rubaiyat* and Edwin Arnold's *The Light of Asia*. St. Denis's philosophical and intellectual orientation was thus aligned with a respected American philosophical and literary tradition and its popular manifestation.

For a dance art to become established in this country, two things were necessary: to interest the American public in it and to overcome the moral prejudice against it. It had to be both attractive and "nice." Then, a cycle had to be initiated in which more people would see dance and like it, more would study it, and more would choose it as a career—thus creating more performers who would in turn introduce it to still more people and continue the cycle.

Ruth St. Denis launched such a cycle. Back in the United States for the 1909-1910 season, she played 108 dates in seventeen cities. Besides the cultural centers (New York, Chicago, Boston, Philadelphia), she danced in New Haven, Poughkeepsie, Columbus, Ohio, Utica, Cleveland, Washington, Baltimore, Plainfield, St. Louis, Cincinnati, Pittsburgh, Rochester, and Buffalo. During the following season she played ninety-nine dates in twenty-five cities—this time going as far as the West Coast. In addition to larger cities, she played such small towns as Pueblo, Colorado, and Chico, California.

It was in Denver, in March 1911, that St. Denis's art touched a young man who would become the third great pioneer of American dance. St. Denis did for Ted Shawn what Nietzsche, Whitman, Beethoven, and Wagner had done for Duncan and what Mary Baker Eddy and the cigarette poster had done for St. Denis. She gave him an ecstatic revelation of what a dance art could be, a revelation that gave shape to his own unfocused yearnings.

Shawn had already seen performances by the ballet dancers Mikhail Mordkin, Anna Pavlova, Gertrude Hoffmann, and Theodore Kosloff. These had stimulated his interest in dance. Seeing the men in particular had encouraged him to pursue dance as a career, but they had "awakened nothing deep" in him. In contrast, seeing St. Denis perform *The Incense* was a profound experience. "I wept, not caring that it was in a crowded theatre—and never before or since, have I known so true a religious experience or so poignant a revelation of perfect beauty. I date my own artistic birth from that night."[17]

It was St. Denis who provided the soul-stirring experience that would give him a grand vision of dance and its mission. And it is most significant that Shawn—in contrast to Duncan and St. Denis— received his revelation from within the field of American dance. He was the first; many others would follow. This is not to say that Shawn and later dancers have not drawn on sources other than dance for ideas and inspiration. They have. But from this time onward, they were not totally dependent on those other sources; more and more stimulation came from the field of dance itself.

By 1911, dance as a modern American art form was beginning to grow at a rate that would become phenomenal by the 1930s. Shawn joined St. Denis in 1914, and together they created Denishawn, an organization that consisted of performing groups and a series of schools. From 1914 until 1931, St. Denis and Shawn, and eventually the Denishawn company, performed and toured extensively. Among others, they attracted Doris Humphrey, Charles Weidman, Martha Graham, and Louis Horst—the leaders of the subsequent development in the new American dance. The regenerative dance cycle begun by Ruth St. Denis was not the only one in twentieth century America. There were later analogous developments in ballet, in the popular theater, and in education. But the progression which began with Ruth St. Denis ended in the establishment of the new and vital art form we call modern dance which would profoundly influence the dance developments in these other areas.

To the partnership with St. Denis, Shawn brought a number of assets. First of all, he brought a religious commitment equal to hers in fervor, but less mystical and otherworldly. A severe illness had interrupted his studies for the Methodist ministry. The dancing that he took up as a way to regain his physical strength eventually replaced the ministry as his chosen career. He has written that this

was not really a change of base at all, it was only a change of form; and when I met Miss St. Denis, we found that our fundamental concept of the dance was the same. She, pursuing the dance upstream to its source, found there religion, and I, pursuing religion upstream, found the dance was the first and finest means of religious expression, and so we have been wedded artistically and humanly ever since. And our whole endeavor is to make possible a school of the dance which works from a spiritual and religious center and which tries to go on creating new forms of the dance—finer, broader and better than any forms have been before.[18]

To the partnership, Shawn also brought a comprehensive knowledge of the types of dance available in America at that time, experience in teaching dance and organizing programs, a well-built body, and a degree of performing skill. He had first studied dance in Denver under Hazel Wallack, once a dancer with the Metropolitan Opera

Ballet. Then he had gone to Los Angeles to broaden his dance experience. There, with Norma Gould, he did exhibition ballroom dancing at the then popular *thés dansants* and organized and presented programs of "classic and interpretive dancing" for clubs and organizations. He also taught and choreographed, and he and Gould formed a small dance company. They appeared in a film called *The Dance of the Ages* which Shawn conceived and directed, then they set off on a tour for the Santa Fe Railroad that took them across the country to New York.

Before settling in New York, Shawn spent a month studying the Delsarte system under Mary Perry King at her Uni-Trinitarian School of Personal Harmonizing and Self-Development in New Canaan, Connecticut. Once in New York he studied Russian, Italian, and French ballet, Spanish dancing, pantomime, and the latest ballroom steps. He began to teach and, with Norma Gould, to perform occasionally. As soon as St. Denis saw him dance, she realized that he was the "best male dancing material in America."

 Another asset brought by Shawn was his strong motivation to create a school of dance far greater in scope than anything America had known up to that time. St. Denis has credited him with being the instigator and driving force behind the Denishawn school:

Ted's conceptive mind in relation to the school was infinitely clearer and stronger than mine. His whole being leaped to an organization which would take care, in its housing and schedules, of those elements of art, those techniques and that culture which we were bursting to give. My part, obviously, would be to supply the atmosphere. My Oriental career and his own former teaching and performing experience were the substance upon which he was to make his design. From first to last the outline and organization of the Denishawn School was Ted's.[19]

The school opened in Los Angeles in the summer of 1915 and continued for about fifteen years. Sometimes it was under the control of one or the other of its founders; sometimes they were both with it. When Shawn and St. Denis were touring, the school was left in the charge of assistants they had trained. Branches were established in other American cities, and the school was eventually based in New York.

Finally, Shawn brought to St. Denis the possibility of greater variety and scope in her programs. To her interest in the Orient he added an interest in Spanish, Greek, Christian, American, and American Indian themes. There were now two choreographers and two star performers to pool their resources and create rich and varied programs with which to entice the American public.

The success of Ruth St. Denis and Ted Shawn is most significant both because of the quantity of their performing activity and because of the modern dance movement which their work triggered. What was it that made St. Denis, and later Denishawn, appealing enough to get such extensive booking and to set the cycle going? Part of the answer has been given by Christena L. Schlundt in her biography of St. Denis. As Schlundt points out, St. Denis's dances were excellent theater, with colorful costumes, sumptuous settings in the popular Belasco style, supernumeraries to provide local color, lovely music, and a skillful handling of contrast and pacing. Within this grand production style, which Schlundt has called operatic, there was St. Denis, "a beautiful woman moving beautifully," who, at the same time exuded an aura of "austere saintliness," and profound mystery. "The dance itself was exotic and sensual; the intent and message were anti-sensual." St. Denis was sensational in her near-nudity, exotic in her themes, and *new*. At the same time, she insisted on the spiritual intent of her work.

St. Denis's popular production style was continued in the Denishawn productions. St. Denis and Shawn knew how to put on a good show in any setting. In addition, they were always willing to compromise their ideals in vaudeville for a good cause—to earn money to support the school and their more serious work. This was eventually to lower their prestige in the eyes of some of their own students. In 1928, right before her break with Denishawn, Doris Humphrey refused to tour with the Ziegfeld Follies to earn money for Denishawn. She told her teacher, "I saw what you did in the Follies, and I was shocked. The dances had been altered, the tempi were much faster, and you, Miss Ruth, had your skirts pulled up four or five inches higher than they should have been."[20] But such compromises started the cycle that would be so fruitful, and they supported the activities of Denishawn throughout its long life. With a more austere and uncompromising attitude, St. Denis and Shawn might not have been able to make the initial breakthrough for American dance.

That St. Denis, and later Denishawn, presented notably attractive programs accounts in part for their appeal and consequent success. But they also had to convince the American public of the moral worth of their art and of the moral rectitude that was as possible for dancers as for any other members of society. They accomplished the first of these by their own religious and spiritual preoccupations. They accomplished the second by leading impeccably proper lives.

St. Denis had considered living with Shawn without formal marriage, and later she felt that perhaps that would have been the better

and more courageous thing to do. But at the time, she could not act so
much against the prevailing moral code. She writes:

I suddenly saw myself in my self-appointed role of guardian of those ten
thousand youngsters who took so many of their ideas and ideals from the
men and women of the stage. I knew that to them I was a woman of the
theater who had no front-page scandals attached to her name, for the simple
reasons that there had been none to record. I wanted to stand for the lofty and
spiritual things in both my life and my art. My spiritual pride was deep and I
did not wish to give up this image that had been created of me. . . . I knew
that any and all sex relationships outside of marriage were classed without
distinction or explanation as sinful and degraded, and of this I was not and
could not be guilty.

Ruth St. Denis and Ted Shawn were married August 13, 1914.[21]

Not only did St. Denis and Shawn live respectable lives; they also
tried to impose the accepted morality on their students and company.
As late as 1928 they were disturbed by "various affairs that had been
going on from time to time" among members of Greater Denishawn
in New York. They felt that these were "questionable, if not down-
right immoral, as they did not result in marriage." So they decided to
initiate a new policy:

A committee of faculty members would be established to hear the evidence in
such cases. Permission to continue would be granted, or marriage would be
advised. If the advice were flouted there would be an instant cessation of the
affair, or the guilty parties would be dismissed at once.[22]

Perhaps Isadora was more courageous in her stand for sexual freedom (and more interesting in the flamboyance of her life), but St.
Denis and Shawn were more useful for the development of the
American dance profession. They proved to the American middle
class that dancers could live by the middle-class moral code. They
established a school and an organization to which no middle-class
mother need fear to send her daughter.

St. Denis and Shawn were also upright in money matters. Duncan
begged money from society ladies and from rich lovers, and she ran
out on debts whenever she found it convenient. In contrast, St. Denis
and Shawn conscientiously worked for every penny they used. Duncan could feel self-righteous because she would not degrade her art
by performing in variety houses; St. Denis and Shawn could feel the
same emotion for paying their debts and paying their own way,
whatever the cost to their artistic pride. Their standards were much
more acceptable in America than were Duncan's.

A third area in which Denishawn pleased and Duncan offended
was their attitudes toward America. Duncan initially slighted her

country by staying away from it. She added insult to injury by a devotion to art so extreme that she was perfectly willing to become a Bolshevik if the Bolsheviks would support her school. Then she married a Russian poet. As a final blow, on visits to America she treated her countrymen with contempt—expecially those who had prestige and power. The press had such a good time with all this that she was anathema by the end of her last visit in 1923.

In contrast, St. Denis and Shawn did nothing to offend and much to please. When the Germans offered to build a theater in honor of St. Denis if she would remain in Germany for five years, she refused— for "underneath all my interests in other cultures and other races I was intensely patriotic and I felt that whatever value my life had should be developed and spent in America."[23] She returned to America after only two years abroad and stayed here except for occasional touring engagements.

When the United States entered World War I in 1917, Shawn enlisted and was assigned to organize entertainment for the army and to sell Liberty Bonds. Eventually, he was corralled for Officers' Training School. In that training program against his will, he was nevertheless "grimly determined to get through," for "failure to earn the commission would bring disgrace not only to me but to my profession as well."[24] Like St. Denis, Shawn always had the image of the dance profession in focus. Both of them were willing to forgo their own desires in the interest of dance.

For her part, St. Denis sold Liberty Bonds, toured vaudeville to buy Liberty Bonds, and entertained the troops. She initiated a course in "useful patriotism" at Denishawn, saying, "Girls who do not want to be patriotic must learn to dance elsewhere." The Shawns had no scruples about imposing their own opinions on others. In addition to the "useful patriotism," which was to include hygiene, first aid, economy, and simple cooking, St. Denis's students were supposed to attend war lectures twice a week, where they would be taught "the democratic principles which forced the United States into the war." One of the school's buildings was given over to the Red Cross Auxiliary, and the school gave benefits and entertainments for the troops. On the last tour to raise money for Liberty Bonds, the program ended with a patriotic pageant called *The Spirit of Democracy*. This piece showed a battle between democracy and autocracy, with democracy achieving a victorious peace at the end.[25]

Before the United States had entered the war, Duncan stirred a New York audience to an emotional peak by her rendition of the *Marseillaise*. But by early 1918 she had returned to Europe and evidenced no interest in America's participation in the war. In contrast, the Shawns identified totally with the American cause, and their support of their country was practical and highly visible.

To sum up, St. Denis, Shawn, and Denishawn enjoyed maximum potential for success with the American public because they were so close in spirit and values to that public. They knew what their audiences enjoyed and were capable of producing it. They actively supported American middle-class values and aspirations with their artistic goals, their morality, their respectability, and their patriotism. They were at all times aware of their responsibility for the public image of dance and dancers.

Denishawn's contributions to the development of American dance have been most significant. Their extensive touring acquainted the populace with dance as an art form and introduced the dance of different cultures to Americans. Their researches into foreign dance arts provided information about the important role that dance has played in other cultures and pointed out the lack of dance as an art in America.

Their emphasis on the spiritual aspects of dance helped break down the moral arguments against it. Their own personal morality and respectability strengthened their position and enhanced the prestige of their profession in America. They added further to its prestige by presenting entire dance programs on the concert stage and by gaining wide recognition for their art in other countries. Shawn made it his personal cause to establish dance as a respectable profession for American men.

Denishawn set the precedent for experimentation with new forms of dance in America. Their innovations included music visualizations, dance without music, dance based on American themes and contemporary themes, and nudity in dance. In this environment of experimentation, they trained the most important subsequent leaders of modern dance: Martha Graham, Doris Humphrey, and Charles Weidman.

Finally, the work of St. Denis and Shawn is significant because of the fervent sense of mission they brought to their art. They, like Duncan, took dance out of the realm of light entertainment and linked it with idealistic goals for humanity. The next generation of dancers—those of the depression years—found it but a short step from the metaphysical goals of Denishawn to the social utopian goals of the 1930s. The modern dance movement has been both blessed and plagued by its persisting sense of mission—its allegiance to goals outside the realm of dance itself.

On the one hand, the sense of mission has helped to legitimize dance in American culture and has justified it in terms of American values. The sense of mission has also provided strong motivation for modern dancers to carry on in an art that—until recent years—has enjoyed neither financial nor popular support. On the other hand, the art of the dance has often been lost in the pursuit of outside goals such as the furtherance of the "revolution," the teaching of democracy, or one or another kind of salvation of mankind.

By the second decade of the twentieth century, the new dance art created by Duncan, St. Denis, and Shawn was established. It was art; it was modern; it was American. It had gained recognition both in the United States and Europe. It was a viable alternative to the old dance art, ballet. A simultaneous and analogous development had occurred in what might be called the revolt against formalism in education— the progressive education movement. In the interim between World War I and the great depression modern dance and modern education came together. Progressive educators were seeking a creative physical activity like the new dance to use in school and college programs. The new theatrical dance was there—to serve as a model for the new educational dance.

NOTES TO CHAPTER 4

1. Friedrich Nietzsche, *Thus Spake Zarathustra*, p. 76.
2. Ruth St. Denis, *An Unfinished Life*, p. 52.
3. Ibid., pp. 16-17.
4. St. Denis letter to Percy Mackaye, in Percy Mackaye, *Epoch: The Life of Steele Mackaye*, II, Appendix II, pp. lvii-lix.
5. St. Denis, *An Unfinished Life*, pp. 9-10.
6. Ibid., p. 40.
7. Ibid., p. 9.
8. Ibid., p. 15.
9. "The Role of Ruth St. Denis in the History of American Dance," p. 44.
10. St. Denis, *An Unfinished Life*, p. 53.
11. Ibid., pp. 46-47.
12. Mary Baker Eddy, *Science and Health with Key to the Scriptures*, p. 170.
13. St. Denis, *An Unfinished Life*, p. 47.
14. Ibid., pp. 51-56.
15. Ibid., pp. 97-98.
16. Gilbert Seldes, *The Stammering Century*, pp. 360-361.
17. Ted Shawn, *Ruth St. Denis*, I, p. 34.
18. Ted Shawn, *The American Ballet*, p. 12.
19. St. Denis, *An Unfinished Life*, p. 172.
20. Doris Humphrey, "New Dance: An Unfinished Autobiography," p. 75.
21. St. Denis, *An Unfinished Life*, pp. 165, 167.
22. Humphrey, "New Dance," p. 74.
23. St. Denis, *An Unfinished Life*, p. 126.
24. Shawn, *One Thousand and One Night Stands*, p. 77.
25. Schlundt, "The Role of Ruth St. Denis," pp. 150-155.

PART II:
The Educational Dance Tradition in America

Above: An *arabesque* turn as taught in Emil Rath's "aesthetic dancing." (From Emil Rath, *Aesthetic Dancing.*)

Right: Gymnastic dancing for men as taught by Staley and Lowery. (From their *Manual of Gymnastic Dancing.*)

CHAPTER 5

Dance in Education: The Eighteenth and Nineteenth Centuries

In contrast to theatrical dance, social and educational dancing has been relatively visible in American history since the colonial period. According to historian Louis B. Wright, "dancing was so prevalent in colonial America that neither Puritans nor Quakers were able to suppress this form of entertainment."[1] The many references to balls, assemblies, and dancing masters that can be found in seventeenth and eighteenth century documents support his statement.

The widespread assumption that the Puritans wished to suppress dancing in New England was proved wrong when music historian Percy Scholes demonstrated that Puritan leaders did not reject all dancing. Many of them danced themselves for pleasure and considered dancing an important part of education for cultivated living. They were, however, discriminating in their attitudes toward dance. They vehemently objected to "mixt" or "gynaecandrical" dancing (men and women dancing in couples), because they considered it a dangerous temptation to sexual misconduct. They also disapproved of dancing around Maypoles because of its pagan connotations, and they opposed dancing coupled with feasting and drinking. What they favored was the popular country dancing in which men and women danced together in formations.

While social dancing existed to some extent in all classes of colonial society, dance as education was emphasized only by the upper class—the bluebloods of the Northern cities and the plantation gentry of the South. The kind of dancing that served their educational purposes was also enjoyed as a social amenity. The ideals of cultivation and the practice of polite dancing were inextricably tied together.

A few dancing masters were already teaching in the colonies by the late seventeenth century, and before long the more worldly members of the Boston community were promoting dancing as a necessary part of their children's education. How else explain Cotton Mather's attack, in 1708, on the money spent for dancing lessons? In a funeral sermon preached on "the Good Education of Children," Mather chided his congregation for underpaying schoolteachers.

Worthy of honour are the Teachers that convey Wisdom unto our children. . . . Their stipends are generally far short of their Deserts. . . . I can't but observe with a just indignation; to *Feed* our Children, to Cloath our Children, to do anything for the Bodies of our Children; or perhaps *to teach them some trifle at a Dancing School,* scarcely worth their learning, we account no expense too much; at the same time to have the Minds of our Children Enriched with the most valuable Knowledge, here, To what purpose? is the cry; a little expense, how heavily it goes off! *My Bretheren, These things ought not so to be.* [2]

To Cotton Mather, dancing was at best a trifle—certainly not a significant part of education. But his parishioners obviously held a different opinion. They continued sending their children to dancing masters and indulging in their own enjoyment of balls and assemblies. Society families in other Northern colonies did the same.

Dancing survived and flourished in Quaker and Puritan areas despite sporadic attacks from moralists and churchmen. In contrast, it flourished in the South with the help—not the hindrance—of the most highly esteemed leaders. Wright tells us that

in the areas where the Anglican faith prevailed, dancing was a part of the social routine on all levels of society and was sometimes carried to excess. . . . To South Carolinians, Virginians, and Marylanders of the upper class, life without balls and "assemblies" would have been regarded as barren and uncivilized. [3]

For the Southern planter, dance was a respected accomplishment. His way of life was particularly hospitable to dance—stressing, as it did, form and graciousness—and his religion was not antagonistic.

Dancing was visibly significant in Southern colonial upper-class culture. But we must keep in mind that dance served a similar function among the colonial aristocrats of the North. For our well-bred colonial forebears, North and South, dancing was an important part of their cultural training.

Most of the information we have about dancing in the colonies comes from diaries and journals. One of the most interesting was written by Philip Vickers Fithian, a young New Jersey man who had studied for the Presbyterian ministry at Princeton. Fithian spent part of 1773 and 1774 as tutor to the children of Robert Carter of Nomini Hall, one of the great plantations of Tidewater Virginia.

Upon arriving at his new post, one of the first persons Fithian met was Francis Christian, an itinerant dancing master who "held his classes in rotation at a number of manor houses of the Northern Neck." This was an appropriate introduction to life at Nomini Hall. Since the plantation society was far more pleasure-loving than what the young tutor had known before, he was at first surprised and somewhat disapproving. But in time he developed misgivings about his own education and upbringing—especially regarding dance. Of one evening when he had been "strongly solicited by the young Gentlemen to go in and dance," he wrote in his diary:

I declined it, however, and went to my Room not without Wishes that it had been a part of my Education to learn what I think is an innocent and an ornamental, and most certainly, in this Province is a necessary qualification for a person to appear even decent in Company.[4]

Fithian's fascination with this exotic activity led him to devote many pages to dancing at Nomini Hall.

The Virginia aristocracy danced on occasions of every sort. At the most informal level were the dances held during the dancing master's visits. Teaching at each plantation for two days at a time, Mr. Christian would give lessons in the mornings and afternoons to the children of the house and to students from neighboring plantations. In the evenings, the adults of the house and their visitors would join the young people in minuets and country dances. Special occasions were celebrated with lavish balls, such as the one given by Squire Richard Lee of Lee Hall in January 1774. This festivity, typical for its time, was planned to last four or five days and was attended by some seventy people. It was an elaborate entertainment with choice food and drink, facilities for various games, and incessant dancing.

The Southern aristocracy promoted dancing as an essential element of education. The tradition of dancing was instilled in each generation by formal training in the art. This was provided by the itinerant dancing masters who traveled from one plantation to another, by urban dancing masters who taught at fixed locations, and by dancing classes within the curriculum of general educational institutions.

Of the itinerant rural dancing masters, we have most information about Francis Christian because he appears in three of the great diaries of the period—those of Fithian, George Washington, and Colonel Landon Carter of Sabine Hill. There is record of Christian from March 13, 1770, when he is first mentioned by Washington, until June 23, 1779, the date of a letter from Robert Carter which dismissed him from employment at Nomini Hall. Carter had adopted the Baptist faith and rejected dancing as a fitting field of study for his children—an example of the relationship between religious belief and attitudes toward dancing.

Fithian provides us with the most information about Christian. From his journal we know that the dancing master was working steadily in the Northern Neck area from October 1773 until October 1774 (the approximate dates of Fithian's tenure at Nomini Hall). Christian's circuit included the large plantations of the area. He taught the children in classes that were held every three or four weeks for two days at a time. Christian seemed to enjoy the same social acceptance among the great families for whom he worked as did Fithian himself. Neither one was relegated to an inferior place in the house. On the contrary, they ate with the families and were included in social activities with what appears to be equal status.

The planter aristocracy took dance education seriously and sought the best teachers for their children. There is evidence that Washington, for example, was far from indifferent to the quality of dance lessons provided for his wards. In 1769 he wrote to Reverend Jonathan Boucher, in whose school his stepson Jacky Custis was enrolled:

In respect to the Dancing Gentry, I am glad to find you have such a choice of them, and that Newman has got the start of his rival Spooner, because I have heard him well spoken of as a teacher in that Science. The others misfortunes might recommend him to the notice & charity of the well disposed, but if his accomplishments in that way are inferior to the others it ought by no means to entitle him to the preference—you will be so good therefore, sir, to enter Mas^{tr} Custis with M^r. Newman for a year or otherwise as he may from his school. [5]

Charles Carter of Cleve, another Virginia aristocrat, was enough concerned about his children's dance training to mention it when he made his will in 1762. He wrote that his sons were to be taught dancing "till they are well accomplished," and that his daughters should be "maintained with great frugality and taught to dance."[6]

That the training was serious and strict we learn from Fithian:

I observed in the course of the lessons, that Mr. Christian is punctual, and rigid in his discipline, so strict indeed that he struck two of the young Misses for a fault in the course of their performance, even in the presence of the Mother of one of them! And he rebuked one of the young Fellows so highly as to tell him he must alter his manner, which he had observed through the Course of the Dance, to be insolent, and wanton, or absent himself from the School—I thought this a sharp reproof, to a young Gentleman of seventeen, before a large number of Ladies![7]

Dancing was as serious a field of study as any other for the planter children. As Fithian said, it was a "necessary qualification for a person to appear even decent in Company."

The dancing culture of the colonial upper classes, north or south, derived from Europe. All the dancing masters came from abroad or had been trained by Europeans. Fashionable dance in America was patterned on fashionable dance in Europe. And the societal and educational values for which dance was seriously appreciated—these also were part of a European heritage. The many dance manuals and treatises from the late seventeenth and eighteenth centuries tell us what dance meant to colonial Americans.

There is evidence that European dance treatises were to be found in eighteenth century America. One for which we have information was left in the estate of Major Robert Beverley I, of Middlesex County, Virginia, when he died in 1734. Listed as "Ye 2nd vol. of ye Dancing Master," this was undoubtedly the work of John Playford, a "leading purveyor of instruction books" in both dancing and music. This had been an extremely popular text in England during the seventeenth and early eighteenth centuries.

Playford's first volume of *The Dancing Master*, which was called *The English Dancing Master* in its first edition, was published in eighteen editions between 1651 and about 1728. The second volume went through four editions, from about 1713 to 1728, and a third volume had two editions, about 1719 and 1727. The subtitle to the first two volumes was "Directions for Dancing Country Dances with the Tunes to each Dance, for the Treble-Violin," and to the third, "The Third Edition, containing 360 of the choicest Old and New Tunes now used at Court, and other Publick Places." This collection of country dances with accompanying music grew from an original 100 tunes to more than 900 by the time the third volume was published. Country dancing was apparently a flourishing activity in England.

Two treatises were owned by the Williamsburg dancing master Charles Stagg, who died in 1736. On the inventory of his possessions were two books on the art of dancing by J. Weaver and J. Essex. The first would have been either the 1706 or the 1710 edition of John Weaver's *Orchesography*, subtitled:

Or the Art of Dancing, By Characters and Demonstrative Figures. Wherin the whole Art is explain'd; with compleat Tables of all the Steps us'd in Dancing, and Rules for the Motions of the Arms, &c Whereby Any Person (who understands Dancing) may of himself learn all manner of Dances. Being An Exact and Just Translation from the French of Monsieur Feuillet.

The second edition had some additional dances. Cyril Beaumont, dance historian and compiler of the bibliography in which this appears, says that Weaver's work is "an excellent translation of Feuillet's *Chorégraphie*," which was published in Paris in 1701.

Stagg's second book was John Essex's *For the Further Improvement of Dancing*, subtitled:

A Treatise of Chorography or ye Art of Dancing Country Dances after A New Character, in which The Figures, Steps, & Manner of Performing are describ'd, & ye Rules Demonstrated in an Easie Method adapted to the Meanest Capacity. Translated from the French of Monsr. Feuillet, and Improv'd wth. many additions . . .

This is a translation of part of Feuillet's *Recueil de Contredances* of 1706 (its second edition). Beaumont says that this work, far from adding to Feuillet, represents less than a tenth of the original, from which Essex reproduced only the simplest steps and dances.

Another manual, listed as Gallini's *Art of Dancing*, appeared in a *Catalogue of Books Belonging to the Charleston Library Society* (1770). Giovanni Andrea Gallini was "Director of the Dances at the Royal Theatre in the Haymarket," according to the title page of the first edition of his *A Treatise on the Art of Dancing*. The Gallini book in the Charleston Library may have been either the *Treatise* or *Critical Observations on the Art of Dancing;* to which was added, "A Collection of Cotillions or French Dances."

Both of Gallini's books include discussions of the history of dance, establishing a continuing tradition from the Greeks and Romans, and discussions of dance in countries other than England, including such faraway places as China. Gallini thus placed the English dance of the period in a broad historical and geographical context. In a chapter entitled "Upon the Air or Port of the Person," in *Critical Observations*, Gallini devotes thirty-three pages to demeanor and how it may be improved by means of dancing. Another chapter treats of the positions and steps of the dances.

The lessons in the *Treatise* are less practical and more theoretical. Thus there is a chapter on "Sundry Requisites for the Perfection of the Art of Dancing" and another that offers "Some Thoughts on the Utility of Learning to Dance, and especially upon the Minuet." In the latter, Gallini stresses that grace, bearing, and social ease result from the mastery of dancing. Both volumes shed light on educational theory and practice as well as dance in colonial times.

We have tangible evidence that Playford's *Dancing Master*, Feuillet's two works in translation, and one or another of the Gallini books found their way to America in the eighteenth century. These books contained collections of dances with descriptions of their steps and accompanying music, a successful system of dance notation, and a historical and theoretical context providing a rationale for the practice of dancing.

According to the social dance historian A. H. Franks, "there is ample evidence to show that the works of John Weaver and Pierre Rameau (in translation) had made the journey from Europe to America with the dancing masters and that many families owned a copy of one or both of them."[8] Franks did not present any of the ample evidence. But if he is right, America was also exposed to some of John Weaver's own historical and theoretical works, such as *Anatomical and Mechanical Lectures upon Dancing* (London, 1721), in which he tried to formulate laws of movement—to put dancing on a scientific basis; or *An Essay Towards An History of Dancing* (London, 1712), which included "Objections Against Dancing" and "Objections Against Dancing Answered"; or *A Small Treatise of Time and Cadence in Dancing* (London, 1706).

If John Essex's translation of Pierre Rameau's *The Dancing Master* (London, 1728; originally *Le Maître á Danser,* Paris, 1725), found its way to this country, America had an elaborately thorough treatise on dance which not only covered dance positions and steps in great detail, but also treated "Of the Manner of Taking off One's Hat and Putting it on Again," "Of the Manner of Behaving Genteely at Formal Balls," and other such subjects.

The direct connection between European dance literature and the dancing masters and dancing public in America is not clear. But it *is* clear that books such as those just mentioned furnished the dancing masters and—perhaps through them or perhaps directly—the dancing public with intellectual underpinnings as well as practical technique. There is no doubt that dancing was considered a necessary accomplishment among upper-class colonial Americans, and the model they emulated was the European dance culture.

Dancing had important educational functions that were highly valued by these educated aristocrats. We have seen that Gallini greatly emphasized the grace, bearing, and social ease to be gained from the study of dancing. Rameau stressed manners, and he spoke for eighteenth century cultivated society on both sides of the Atlantic:

For dancing must not be regarded as an exercise designed solely for pleasure. I certainly think that the joy and vivacity attendant on banquets and festivals led to its birth, but . . . men have sought to turn to useful account what was originally intended as a diversion. . . . Dancing adds graces to the gifts which nature has bestowed upon us, by regulating the movements of the body and setting it in its proper positions. And, if it do not completely eradicate the defects with which we are born, it mitigates or conceals them.[9]

In Rameau's view, nature provided defects as well as gifts to man—but civilized cultivation, in the form of dance, could enhance the gifts and ameliorate the defects. What a contrast to the view of the late nineteenth century Delsartians, who argued that it was civilized culture that had created defects in man, and that he could remove them only by rediscovering natural ways of moving.

One did not have to be a dancing master to appreciate the educational benefits of dancing in the seventeenth or eighteenth centuries. Philip Dormer Stanhope, Earl of Chesterfield, wrote: "Now to acquire a graceful air, you must attend to your dancing; no one can either sit, stand, or walk well, unless he dances well.[10]

Gallini quoted John Locke, who judged the values of dancing even more highly:

Nothing appears to me to give children so much becoming confidence and behaviour, and so to raise them to the conversation of those above their age as dancing . . . for though this consists only in outward gracefulness of motion, yet I know not how, it gives children manly thoughts and carriage more than any other thing.[11]

And the artist William Hogarth maintained:

There is no one but would wish to have it in his power to be genteel and graceful in the carriage of his person. . . . The usual methods relied on for this purpose among well-bred people, take up a considerable part of their time: even those of the first rank have no other recourse in these matters, than to dancing-masters and fencing-masters.

Inherent in all such statements is the high value that these people placed on form. Dance is form, which makes it both pleasing in itself and effective in instilling a sense of form into life. Ideally, one's life was expected to possess the attributes of the art of dancing. "Grace in action," wrote Hogarth, "depends upon the same principles as have been shown to produce it in forms": fitness, proportion, simplicity, line, and so on.[12] Grace in action was expected whether inside or outside the ballroom. Dancing provided an effective training for life in polite society. It was thus predominantly cultural training in the eighteenth century.

Social dancing of many varieties has continued in popularity up to the present day. And some parents have continued to provide social dance training for their children as a means of teaching them good form. By the turn of the century the accomplishments to be gained from such training—grace, poise, manners, good posture—ceased being the exclusive property of the wealthy or the social elite. As this country democratized, aspirations once held only by the select few finally filtered down and became of some value among the growing middle class. That this process also changed the values attached to dancing is a matter of course. Ann Barzel has written that the numerous German dancing masters who came to the United States after 1870 "attracted large classes of children to whom they taught cotillions and a vague type of work related to ballet. The latter was to make the pupils graceful and was not meant as training for the stage. These fancy dances were exhibited at the balls given by dancing academies and at charity functions."[13] St. Denis's teacher, Karl Marwig, was just such a dancing master.

During most of the nineteenth century, however, social dance training remained within the realm of upper-class culture, and only expensive private schools or institutions like West Point included it in their curriculum. In the years following independence, as education became more widespread, the great task was to teach basic intellectual skills—reading, writing, and arithmetic—to the growing American citizenry. Educators had neither time nor facilities to teach such niceties as grace, form, and polish. In any case, there was something aristocratic, undemocratic, perhaps even un-American about such cultivation. When dancing finally did come into American public schools on a wide scale, it was as "democratic" physical education, not as an aristocratic cultural education.

Interest in physical education in America appeared in the 1820s and became widespread after mid-century. Actual dancing played only a peripheral role in the first surge of the physical education movement—its gymnastic phase—but quasi-dance forms played quite a large role. In time a new kind of dancing developed out of gymnastics and what was called gymnastic dancing, but it had educational and social objectives quite different from those of the eighteenth century dance forms.

The first stage of the physical education movement in America, which lasted through the early 1830s, included four kinds of activities: military exercises and marching, manual labor as exercise, the German or Jahn system of gymnastics, and a form of calisthenics developed particularly for women. Only the last two are relevant here.

Jahn gymnastics was introduced into America in various settings. The historian of physical education Fred Eugene Leonard writes:

The first school, college, and public gymnasia in the United States—all of them outdoor ones of the early Jahn type—were opened in the years 1825 and 1826 in Massachusetts, at Northhampton, Cambridge, and Boston. All three were laid out and directed by university trained Germans, who had been active participants in the Jahn gymnastics in their student days and had left their native land for the United States in order to escape arrest or constant persecution under the reactionary policy adopted by the Holy Alliance.[14]

In the late eighteenth century, French political refugees of the right, fleeing the revolution, had brought us dance. In the early nineteenth century, German political refugees of the left, fleeing reactionary repression, brought us gymnastics. As one might expect, the dance that eventually developed out of the gymnastics movement would be much more liberal in all its characteristics than the aristocratic dance that had first served educational ends in America.

Jahn's system, which required gymnasia equipped with heavy apparatus, included "walking, running, jumping, vaulting the horse, balancing, the horizontal bar, the parallel bars, climbing, throwing, pulling, pushing, lifting, carrying, holding the body outstretched horizontally, wrestling, jumping with the hoop and with the rope, and miscellaneous exercises," and various gymnastic games. Jahn described all these in his treatise on gymnastics (1816). An English adaptation of this work was published in Northampton, Massachusetts, eight years later.

A second and larger influx of German refugees began in 1848— again brought about by political turmoil and the subsequent reactionary crackdown in Germany. These immigrants established *Turnvereine*—gymnastics clubs—wherever they settled. By the Civil War there were some 150 local clubs with about 10,000 members. The *turner* movement declined temporarily during the Civil War, but interest began to grow once more after the war. In 1866 a training school for teachers was established in New York City; it was transferred to Milwaukee in 1874.

Until 1866, the *turner* activity had been by and for German-Americans. But from then on the leaders began a campaign to introduce the Jahn system more widely. They accomplished this with demonstrations and papers presented to the Association for the Advancement of Physical Education, with books written about the system in English, and with classes offered to the general public. Before the close of the century, physical education was introduced into many public schools by graduates of the Normal School of the *Turnerbund*.

Jahn himself had not included dancing in his system. But after 1865, dancelike exercises were introduced in the American *Turnvereine*, including "skipping, change stepping, follow-stepping, galloping, and a few other fundamental steps, with variations." These probably derived from the rhythmic gymnastics that had entered the German system after Jahn.

Another European gymnastics system was introduced into America in the second half of the nineteenth century. This was the Swedish or Ling system, which comprised two parts. The first, consisting of medical gymnastics (exercises to effect cures), was known in this country as early as the 1850s. Then a Ling system of educational gymnastics was introduced into America in the 1880s in Boston, the patron city of physical culture movements in nineteenth century America.

Books about the Swedish system began to appear in the 1890s. One of these was written by Hartvig Nissen, director of the Swedish Health Institute in Washington and teacher of Ling gymnastics at Johns Hopkins, Harvard, the Boston public schools, and other insituations. In *The ABC of Swedish Educational Gymnastics* (1891), Nissen gives a clear statement of the goals and methods of the system:

1. to develop the body and produce strength and health,
2. by increasing the strength of the body and by endurance and skill to develop freshness of mind, powerful will, resoluteness and courage, and
3. to assist the school in its educational work by making the pupil accustomed to strict attention, quick and exact execution of given orders; to master his own will and to subordinate himself as part of a great totality.

The Swedish gymnastics were systematized into increasingly difficult and taxing progressions. There were three categories of exercises done in each "day's order": order and marching exercises, gymnastic exercises of separate parts of the body, and gymnastic games which consisted of running, pulling ropes, and dancing. Commands were given for each exercise in a terse, staccato, military manner.

Besides the popular imported gymnastics, two physical training systems were developed by nineteenth century Americans. These were designed not for the male athlete, but for women, children, and nonathletic men—in other words, for general public physical education.

First to appear was the system of Catherine Beecher, sister of Harriet Beecher Stowe. Beecher was one of the major early promoters of women's education in America. In her girls' seminary in Hartford, Connecticut (founded 1823), and in her Western Female Institute in Cincinnati (founded 1834), Beecher set aside half an hour a day for the calisthenics she had developed for her students.

Beecher said of her system that it was "so combined with music and constantly varying evolutions as to serve as an amusement and also as a mode of curing distortions, particularly all tendencies to curvature of the spine; while at the same time it tends to promote grace of movement and easy manners."[15] She compared her system with contemporary gymnastics and found it superior because it needed no special room or apparatus; it involved no danger "either from *excess* or from *accidents*"; it was appropriate and effective for both men and women; it was based on scientific principles, drawing from "most of what is to be found in the French and English works that exhibit the system of *Ling*, the celebrated Swedish Professor, whose method has been widely adopted in European schools and universities"; and finally, it was "so illustrated by drawings, and so exactly arranged as to mode and time, that *any* person, young or old, can practice it without aid from a teacher."[16]

Beecher's calisthenics were described as resembling dancing, but she did not consider them that. She saw her system as "a far more efficient means than dancing, for improving the form and the manners, without any of its evils." Beecher insisted that her system provided the same benefits that the dancing masters had claimed for dancing in the previous century: It taught form, grace, manners; and it was remedial and recreational. But she would not, or could not, call it dancing. One wonders whether she really considered her calisthenics quite different from dancing or whether she made the distinction because society was then unwilling to accept the idea of dancing in a serious educational framework.

In 1832, Beecher published *Course of Calisthenics for Young Ladies*, but more influential, according to physical education historian Van Dalen, was her work of 1856, *A Manual of Physiology and Calisthenics for Schools and Families*. From this time, she worked energetically for the introduction of physical education into all American schools.

Dio Lewis was the other important mid-century promoter of a variety of gymnastics designed especially for nonathletes. This former school teacher, medical student, and lecturer on women's rights and temperance called his system the "New Gymnastics" and first presented it in 1860 to a meeting of the American Institute of Instruction at Boston. The secretary of this organization wrote, "It was regarded as one of the most important and practically valuable subjects which has come before the meetings of this Institute." The Institute recommended that Lewis's gymnastics be introduced into all schools and for general use. A number of schools subsequently incorporated his system into their programs.

Lewis opened a Normal Institute for Physical Education in Boston in 1861. It lasted until late in that decade and graduated at least 250 students who went on to teach in girls' schools and women's colleges.

This was the first successful physical education teacher training institute in the United States.

In 1862 Lewis published a treatise on his system, *The New Gymnastics for Men, Women, and Children*. The similarities between his approach and Beecher's are striking. According to Van Dalen, Lewis culled his exercises from many sources, including Catherine Beecher. Like Beecher, Lewis stressed that his exercises were adaptable to anyone with any degree of strength, that they did not require heavy, fixed apparatus and could thus be done anywhere. Like her, he frowned on dancing for exercise, arguing that

dancing, to say nothing of its almost inevitably mischievous concomitants, brings into play chiefly that part of the body which is already in comparative vigor, and which, besides, has less to do directly, with the size, position and vigor of the vital organs.

Lewis also recommended that his gymnastics be accompanied by music.

Exercises with the upper extremities are as much improved by music as those with the lower extremities. Indeed with the former there is much more need of music, as the arms make no noise, such as might secure concert in exercise with the lower extremities.

A small drum, costing perhaps $5, which may be used as a bass drum, with one beating stick, with which one may keep time, is, I suppose, the sort of music most classes in gymnastics will use at first. And it has advantages. While it is less pleasing than some other instruments, it secures more perfect concert than any other.

The violin and piano are excellent, but on some accounts the hand-organ is the best of all.

Feeble and apathetic people, who have little courage to undertake gymnastic training, accomplish wonders under the inspiration of music. I believe five times as much muscle can be coaxed out, under this delightful stimulus, as without it.[17]

Lewis used music to provide a common beat and to spur the students on to more energetic effort. This was getting close to dance—not as the eighteenth century defined it, but rather as it would appear in the twentieth century.

Where Lewis differed appreciably from Beecher was in the goals he sought. Making no mention of grace, form, or manners, he stressed purely physical benefits, described in quasi-medical fashion. He demanded of exercises that they "make the form erect, and the shoulders and chest, large and vigorous." He severely criticized exercises that did not, in his opinion, correct slumping shoulders. He argued for flexibility over strength, and particularly sought to effect "an elastic, vigorous condition of the nervous system," believing it necessary for the proper functioning of the organs. Lewis summed up the argument for his system in these words:

All persons of both sexes, and of every age, who are possessed of average vitality, should, in the department of physical education, employ light apparatus, and execute a great variety of feats, which require skill, accuracy, courage, dash, presence of mind, quick eye and hand—in brief, which demand a vigorous and complete exercise of all the powers and faculties with which the Creator has endowed us.[18]

He designed his system to accomplish these ends. There is no taint of aristocratic ornament in Lewis's gymnastics. It is all practical and straightforward physical education for physical and mental health.

By the end of the 1860s, physical education was becoming an important element in American education. The first teacher training schools had begun to do their work. Boston was established as the center of the physical education movement. The growth in educational facilities for both men and women had created a need for more and more teachers, and the field was expanding.

Beginning in the 1880s, new kinds of dance began to enter the mainstream of physical education. In 1887 Dr. William G. Anderson, a leading physical training educator, began to teach dancing at his own Brooklyn Normal School for Physical Education, at the Chautauqua School of Physical Education (a summer school), and later at Yale and other schools. He did this because he felt that "dancing could be used to arouse greater interest in gymnastics" and that "the right kind of dancing would develop the ear, as well as add to the grace of [his] students." The first dance he taught was a straight jig. In their manual and history of gymnastic dancing, S. C. Staley and D. M. Lowery tell us that Anderson had

studied and quite thoroughly learned Russian ballet dancing, Irish jigs, reels, and clogs, and while traveling in the south, learned some breakdowns and negro clogs. He also learned buck-and-wing and soft shoe dancing in Holland and England and some in this country.

Anderson told these authors that he taught all these dances in his various physical education classes.

Also important in the early development of gymnastic dancing was Dr. Dudley A. Sargent—teacher, writer, administrator, and promoter of physical education in American higher education. In 1887 Sargent engaged Christian Eberhard, director of the Boston *Turnverein*, to teach dance at the Harvard Summer School of Physical Education. They called the course "fancy step" to avoid criticism from churchmen. It included change steps, schottische, touch steps, waltz, and mazurka. These dance steps had been done in the *Turnvereine* for years, but this was the first time they were introduced widely to the non-German population and presented with Anglicized names.

In 1894 Sargent introduced aesthetic calisthenics (also known as dancing calisthenics, aesthetic dance, or classic dance) into his own normal school as well as at Harvard. As developed and taught by Melvin Ballou Gilbert, under the direction of Sargent, this sytem consisted of ballet dancing with the *pointe* work removed and with arm and torso movements added. Although originally designed for all ages and both sexes, Gilbert's system was so soft and graceful that men were uninterested in it and unwilling to do it, but it became the basis for many physical education programs for women. This was the first time that an established dance system had been adapted specifically for educational use. Many physical education teachers came to Harvard to study the new dance and the methods of teaching it.

Folk and national dances became important in physical education around the turn of the century. They found an enthusiastic supporter in Luther H. Gulick, another leading physical education leader of the late nineteenth and early twentieth centuries. As president of the American Physical Education Association, Gulick chose dancing as the theme for the association's 1905 New York convention. Not only did Gulick present a paper on dancing and rhythm education, but he scheduled three other meetings entirely devoted to dance. These included papers on folk dance and on Gilbert's aesthetic dance as well as demonstrations of folk and national dances. The response was enthusiastic, and folk dance in particular became a fad in the schools for the next few years. Gulick continued his untiring promotion of folk dancing in education, and as the first physical education director of the New York City public schools, his influence was great. In 1910 he published *The Healthful Art of Dancing* in support of the same cause.

Gymnastic dance persisted until well into the twentieth century although it was nineteenth century in essence. There continued to be different systems for men and women. For the women, Gilbert's work was continued by Emil Rath, director of the Normal College, North American Gymnastic Union, Indianapolis. The benefits Rath claimed for his aesthetic dancing concerned the maintenance and improvement of health. He advocated dancing for endurance and coordination as well as to increase heart activity, circulation, respiration, and metabolism. These were traditional arguments for a gymnastic activity. But Rath also struck a new note: the artistic satisfaction to be gained from dancing.

Dancing is rapidly becoming a universal and popular art-form of expression.

. . . This new spirit seems destined to burst the prosaic bonds of our present day materialism, by giving the inner life of the people a medium for artistic expression based upon universal, age-old, all-permeating rhythm—dancing in its various forms. [19]

This kind of argument would dominate modern educational dance rationale during the 1920s.

Rath's book, *Aesthetic Dancing,* is a practical manual for teachers. Ballet steps are described individually, the commands to be called out (a holdover from conventional gymnastics) are given, the rhythm of the steps is added, and appropriate arm movements are suggested. Finally, individual steps are combined into sequences for various tempos including the waltz, the schottische, and the polka.

Gymnastic dancing as it developed for men and boys is treated in Staley and Lowery's *Manual of Gymnastic Dancing.* Published in 1920, this work is the revision of Staley's thesis written for the YMCA College of Springfield, Massachusetts, in 1917. The work includes a history of gymnastic dancing beginning with the Greeks; a section on dance in education; other sections on teaching methods, the use of music, compiling dances, and nomenclature; and sample dances for preliminary, elementary, intermediate, and advanced grades.

Staley's work begins with the difference between aesthetic and gymnastic dance. The first, he maintains, "implies grace, complexity, and femininity," while the second "implies vigor, simplicity, and masculinity." He defines gymnastic dances as folk or national dances "modified to meet the demands of the men's gymnasium class" and says that they were being used in physical training departments of Amherst, Yale, Pennsylvania, Columbia, Cornell, and other universities; leading schools and summer schools of physical education; and secondary schools, *Turnvereine,* and YMCAs.

In discussing the goals to be sought and the advantages to be gained from gymnastic dance, Staley concentrates heavily on the maintenance and improvement of health. This is familiar ground; but, like Rath, Staley offers more modern arguments as well. For example, he quotes Luther Gulick's assertion that folk and national dances beneficially recapitulate man's neuromuscular history because they imitate human occupations such as sowing, hunting, and building. The dancer, according to this theory, experiences movements of his more primitive ancestors and the feelings that accompanied them. Staley writes: "Modern psychology advances the theory that children live their fullest lives when they recapitulate the experience of the race. If this is so, there is nothing we can do that would be of as much value as the simple folk dance." [20] This idea was

introduced by G. Stanley Hall, an American psychologist and educator. Hall's *Educational Problems* is the only book on education theory
in Staley's bibliography, and Staley quotes Hall frequently throughout the *Manual*.

Another concern that Staley plays upon to justify gymnastic dance
is over the ill effects of modern life. "The coarseness of man's activities in the commercial, industrial, and athletic pursuits," Staley
tells us, "is softened through his engagement in the group dance."
He believes that respect for one's fellow men is inherent in group
dancing and can be carried over into the business world. Furthermore, dancing can instill group cohesion, because "the group
dance, next to war, is the greatest single factor in uniting people."

Finally, Staley argues that gymnastic dance is esthetically rewarding because of its beauty, its expression of the soul, its universality,
and its ability to elevate man to higher ideals. It is psychologically
rewarding because it "gives rise to the spirit of freedom and play,
having the happy effect of taking the mind far away from immediate
and material worries." He says that even older businessmen in the
gymnasium lose themselves in dance, becoming vigorous and
shouting. Amusing photographs are distributed throughout the
book, but they show none of this abandon.

The Manual of Gymnastic Dancing is a tract aimed at converting
everyone to dance. In its long section on teaching methods, Staley
tries to instill a sense of mission into teachers. Quoting William
Skarstrom, physical education teacher at Wellesley, Staley lists all the
admirable qualities a teacher should possess. He urges the teacher to
develop these traits in order to "realize his highest calling of 'Life
Sharer.' "

We find in Staley an enthusiasm for dance that reminds us of
Duncan and St. Denis. We also find in his book most of the preoccupations of the progressive educators of his day. At the same time, he
is espousing a kind of dance that belongs more to nineteenth century
gymnastics than to twentieth century modern dance, whether educational or professional. He is a transitional figure, connected in
practice to the past and in rationale to the present and the future.

NOTES TO CHAPTER 5

1. *The Cultural Life of the American Colonies,* p. 190.
2. Quoted in Percy Alfred Scholes, *The Puritans and Music in England and New England,*
   p. 65.
3. *The Cultural Life,* pp. 190-191.

4. *Journal and Letters*, p. 43.
5. Quoted in Rupert Hughes, *George Washington*, II, p. 94.
6. "The Will of Charles Carter of Cleve," pp. 62-63.
7. Fithian, *Journal and Letters*, p. 44.
8. *Social Dance: A Short History*, pp. 117-118.
9. *The Dancing Master*, p. xii.
10. *Principles of Politeness*, p. 17.
11. *Treatise*, pp. 13-14.
12. *The Analysis of Beauty*, pp. 225, 277.
13. "European Dance Teachers in the United States," pp. 67-68.
14. *A Guide to the History of Physical Education*, p. 231.
15. Quoted in Dorothy S. Ainsworth, *The History of Physical Education in Colleges for Women*, p. 4.
16. "Calisthenics," in Goodsell, *Pioneers of Women's Education in the United States*, pp. 223-224.
17. Dio Lewis, *The New Gymnastics for Men, Women, and Children*, pp. 13-14.
18. Ibid., p. 69.
19. *Aesthetic Dancing*, pp. iv-vi.
20. Staley, *Manual of Gymnastic Dancing*, p. 31.

CHAPTER 6

Invitation to the Dance: Progressive Education Theory

The value of physical education was recognized here and there in America from the early days of the republic, and a few private schools had even incorporated some form of it into their programs. After the mid-nineteenth century, however, physical education innovators and promoters stimulated much more interest in the field. They argued the value of physical training, developed systems, trained teachers, and worked in any way possible to convince the public and other educators of its worth. At the same time, general education theory reflected a growing commitment to the broadening of educational goals and programs. The eventual incorporation of physical education in school programs—and later, dance in physical education—was made possible by the development and acceptance of educational theories that favored it.

Social evolutionary theories that would lead to Social Darwinsim were introduced into America by the English philosopher Herbert Spencer. The historian of progressive education Lawrence A. Cremin has written that from 1850 onward, Spencer's writings—especially his book on education—achieved great popularity in this country. His influence reached a peak in 1882, when he visited America on a lecture tour.

Spencer believed that men's lives were controlled by the evolutionary process in nature—that the mind itself slowly changed. Such ideas led him to a theory of education as preparation for living in the world as it is—rather than as training for the world as it was, or for the world as it ideally should be. He assigned the highest value to education especially designed for assisting in man's adaptation to his environment. Spencer classified the goals of men in the order of their importance. Self-preservation came first, followed by child rearing, "maintenance of proper social and political relations," and finally, "those miscellaneous activities which make up the leisure part of life, devoted to the gratifications of the tastes and feelings." The ideal education, Spencer believed, would prepare men for each of these ends.

In his thoughts on physical education, Spencer argued that man in his physical nature is an animal and should be as well cared for and trained as any other valuable beast. He must have shocked his contemporaries when he wrote:

It is time that the benefits which our sheep and oxen have for years past derived from the investigations of the laboratory, should be participated in by our children. Without calling in question the great importance of horse-training and pig-feeding, we would suggest that, as the rearing of well-grown men and women is also of some moment, the conclusions indicated by theory, and endorsed by practice, ought to be acted on in the last course as in the first. [1]

Spencer then dealt at length with the basics of an adequate physical education, which he considered to mean not merely physical activity classes, but healthful food and clothing as well. "The ordinary treatment of children . . . errs in deficient feeding; in deficient clothing; in deficient exercise (among girls at least); and in excessive mental application." [2] He believed that education should rectify these errors.

Spencer made a strong case for the broadening of educational goals. One could easily justify physical education—or even dance—in terms of his criteria. Later, dance would be promoted for health and physical fitness (self-preservation), for social adjustment, and for art and recreation. Spencer's theory thus helped open the minds of educators to new concerns such as the importance of physical education. But Spencer himself recommended no formalized physical training program. On the contrary, he argued against gymnastics as being artificial and unnecessary. He believed that superior exercise could be gained from unrestrained play.

The idea of education for adaptation was carried further by the American psychologist and educator G. Stanley Hall, who applied the principles of Darwinsim to the study of psychology. According to Cremin, Hall's influence—from his writings and his leadership as president of Clark University—was felt throughout the nation.

Hall's education theory was based on these postulations: The psychic life and behavior of the individual recapitulates the evolution of the race from pre-savagery to civilization, and each stage is the prerequisite for the achievement of the next. It followed that education should provide experience relating to each stage in this evolution so that each individual could reach the level of civilization. Thus spoke science! Acceptance of these beliefs led to a widespread child-study movement to find out more about children and the stages they supposedly recapitulated. Educators sought to design programs that would reinforce the natural process. In traditional education, the school had been the absolute standard by which the student was judged. The emphasis now shifted to the needs of the student (as determined by the child-studiers), and the school was judged on how far it could meet those needs. According to Cremin, this new point of view "opened the pedagogical floodgates to every manner of activity, trivial as well as useful, that seemed in some way to minister to the 'needs of children.' "[3]

Hall leaves no doubt about the place of dance in his education theory. In *Educational Problems* (1911) he defines dancing as "the liberal, humanistic culture of the emotions by motions," calling it "the best of all illustrations of harmony between mind and body." Hall favors spontaneity rather than formalism in dance.

Although it may become a highly technical art, dancing is best conceived as an originally spontaneous muscular expression of internal states, primarily not with the pupose of imparting, but for the pleasure of expressing them. Thus the pedagogic value of dancing is to enlarge the emotional life by making all the combinations of movements that it is mechanically possible for the body to make.[4]

With this, he has made a subtle distinction between imparting and expressing, two actions that the Delsartians would have considered the same. Hall believed in dancing for personal experience rather than as a medium of communication or theater. Later, dance educators would write of expression as Hall defined the term, but they would nevertheless teach dance as a performing art.

Hall advocated all kinds of dancing and offered many arguments for its value, but as we shall see, most of his reasons stem from the recapitualtion theory. He greatly prized folk and national dances because he believed them to be "moral, social, and aesthetic forces, condensed expressions of ancestral and racial traits" and "marvelous embodiments of the ethical, religious, and in general the temperament of peoples." He maintained that "such action rituals . . . shape as well as utter the very psychic types of the people who developed and were developed by them." He found the performing of folk dances valuable for modern education for the following reasons:

If thinking is evolved out of actions needful for survival, it is such activities as these that contribute to the very temper and tempo of the thought and thus do very much for sane and effective thinking by laying down its neural bases. Hence they give to the individual wholesome feelings and ideas, and weld him to his race, place him in the proper setting to it, endow him with his heritage, and thus integrate him with it.

Hall also recommended imitative dances, whether from traditional folk forms or newly created. In imitating nature, he wrote, the child

participates in the life of plants, flowers, and trees, and feels more keenly the power of the rocks, mountains, sea, sun, moon, storm, morning, evening, and thus restores . . . the now too often lost appreciation of nature, every item of which has sometime and somewhere been an object of worship, and lay deep and betimes a basis of the love of the world, of man, and of God. . . . Here again the child is becoming a key to unlock the secrets of the stages of the development of the race, and vice versa, racial history sheds light upon individual development.

He felt that children should imitate work movements in dance for neuromuscular experiences that derived from more primitive stages of human culture. Work dances were additionally useful, he felt, to

give a vast variety of exercises for face and voice, and circulation of the muscles, . . . implant early a deep, all-sided sympathy for labor and the high arts of human life which makes the best possible basis for an education which is truly liberal if, as we are now learning, industry is the law of culture.[5]

Hall recognized that dancing had been connected with all the profound experiences of life in traditional societies. He felt that educational dance should include religious dances, love dances, and war dances because he believed them capable of "playing upon our muscles in idealized situations and preforming the soul by determining how it will act when these passions are at their acme." Finally, he felt that the acting out of history and mythology in dance would give students a direct experience of past human culture.

Hall did not limit his recommendations to formalized and imitative dances. He also argued for free and unstructured dancing for emotional expression and physical and psychological release. Feelings that are not evoked or not permitted in ordinary life could by this means be experienced and expressed. This he felt would provide a safety valve for the emotions, lead to psychic health, and enrich the dancer's emotional life.

Hall attributed additional salutary benefits to dancing: It enriches human communication and makes it more truthful; it enhances the appreciation of music; it strengthens the body and develops muscular control; and it expresses things that cannot be expressed with words.

His enthusiasm is so great that he seems to be offering dance as a panacea for all the world's ills.

As a practical analysis of what benefits dance can bring to the modern world, Hall's chapter on dance is overly optimistic. Can educational dance really integrate the student with his cultural heritage and re-establish his contact with nature and with his own emotions? Can it reverse the trend of alienation in the modern world? In cultures where dancing is performed regularly from childhood onward and is an integral part of the society's rituals and festivities, it probably does bestow many of the benefits Hall has claimed for it. Such societies are still relatively traditional and unified, and dancing may help preserve that state for them.

American culture has in contrast always been extremely heterogeneous, and dance has at best been a peripheral activity. Dance expression has been so far from the center of everyday life for the average person that it has had no chance to serve the general population as Hall would have liked. At best, it can serve the minority who develop a special interest in it.

As propaganda for dance, on the other hand, Hall's chapter was excellent. Like Staley's book on gymnastic dance, it is a tract aimed at convincing educators of the great value of dance in education. Hall is comparable to Isadora Duncan in his great love of dance and his faith in its potentialities. Where he differs from her is in the intellectual and scientific pretensions with which he approaches the subject.

What Duncan sensed intuitively, Hall discussed scientifically and academically. His science may now be old-fashioned and quaint, but during the formative years of progressive education—from the 1890s onward—he was a leading figure in both education and psychology. Hall's chapter on dance is thus the statement of a highly respected scholar at the height of his career. He supported his claims for dance with historical evidence and with the latest psychological and educational theory. By 1910 American prejudice against dance had decreased enough that this respected intellectual leader could without embarrassment advocate its practice. That Hall did this—and did it so well—lessened the prejudice even more and enhanced the prestige of dance in American education.

Hall—like Staley, who relies so heavily on his ideas—is a transitional figure. His theories also point both backward and forward. As noted earlier, they served to justify gymnastic dance—a nineteenth century form. They provided a strong rationale for pure folk dancing—which attained greater and greater acceptance in education after the turn of the century. Finally, they pointed the way for the modern educational dance that was to come. Hall suggested many of the actual ideas of that dance and the rationales that would be used to justify them.

Both Spencer and Hall saw the human being as a passive creature acted upon by his environment. They believed education should reinforce the natural evolutionary process and help people adapt to what was. This point of view was opposed by the pragmatists, led by William James and John Dewey. These philosophers did not deny evolution, but they believed that we have some control over the development of the environment. Education, they said, should teach us how to manipulate and control our world; it should work to the ends of social reform and progress. If there is one idea that stands out in the thought of subsequent education theorists and dance educators, it is this. Belief in the efficacy of progressive education in curing the world's ills is present in much of their writing.

Dewey recognized the need for physical education in school, and it was included in the curriculum of his Laboratory School in Chicago. But it was not with his physical education theory or practice that Dewey affected the development of educational dance. His ideas on the subject were no more advanced than those of Spencer or Dio Lewis. Physical education at the Laboratory School included sports, games, and active play (the Spencerian formula); rhythmic drills, both with and without wands and dumbbells; remedial exercises (the Lewis canon); and sometimes fencing for girls. According to Mayhew and Edwards in their history of the Laboratory School, the physical education department barely got into "the art of rhythmic movement as now developed in the esthetic and interpretative dance." Only "in the last year of the school . . . the first steps toward such a development were taken."[6]

Dewey's physical education theory and practice may have given nothing new to physical education or to educational dance, but his general education theory was used extensively to shape as well as to justify physical education and educational dance programs. One can hardly find a book on either subject that does not acknowledge his influence. In writing of the effect of philosophy on physical education, for example, Elwood Craig Davis says that twentieth century physical education programs reflect the spirit of Dewey's educational philosophy. Frederick Rand Rogers, leading physical educator and advocate of dance in education, says that John Dewey dominates the theme of his *Educational Objectives of Physical Education.* Margaret H'Doubler, pioneer of dance education, and Alma Hawkins, prominent dance educator a generation later, both include Dewey in their bibliographies and draw heavily on his ideas in their texts.

Which of Dewey's ideas did the physical educators and dance

educators find useful? It was his contention that education in a democracy should be education *for* democracy.

In 1899, Dewey advised an audience of parents and educators to make of each school

an embryonic community life, active with types of occupations that reflect the life of the larger society and permeated throughout with the spirit of art, history, and science. When the school introduces and trains each child of society into membership within such a little community, saturating him with the spirit of service, and providing him with the instruments of effective self-direction, we shall have the deepest and best guaranty of a larger society which is worthy, lovely, and harmonious. [7]

Schools should thus train the students to live effectively and harmoniously in the larger community and make the community better. Since American society was organized on democratic principles, the schools must work to instill self-direction in the pupils.

Dewey elaborated this idea fifteen years later. In a democracy, he said, "the conventional type of education which trains children to docility and obedience, to the careful performance of imposed tasks because they are imposed," was out of place because it did not prepare for the responsibility of self-government. Furthermore, it actually worked against the complete realization of the democratic ideal:

If we train our children to take orders, to do things simply because they are told to, and fail to give them confidence to act and think for themselves, we are putting an almost insurmountable obstacle in the way of overcoming the present defects of our system and of establishing the truth of democratic ideals. . . . Children in school must be allowed freedom so that they will know what its use means when they become the controlling body, and they must be allowed to develop active qualities of initiative, independence, and resourcefulness, before the abuses and failures of democracy will disappear. [8]

Dewey had articulated his ideal; educators of all kinds experimented with ways of achieving it. Among them were the physical educators, who searched for new approaches in their own field that would be less formal, artificial, and authoritarian than gymnastics and gymnastic dance. One of the activities thus developed was educational modern dance. From the beginning, it was seen as an activity more appropriate to democratic America than nineteenth century physical training systems had been.

Jesse Feiring Williams, a noted physical education leader and enthusiastic promoter of the new dance, articulated the new point of view most clearly. In his foreword to Agnes L. and Lucile Marsh's *The Dance in Education* (1924), Williams wrote:

Among certain European nations where militaristic aims govern educational practice, and achievements of the human personality are sacrificed to political considerations, the training for military ends shapes physical education inevitably toward mass exercises and calisthenic drills. . . .

Modern physical education in America is rapidly getting away from this type, long ago introduced here by foreign refugees and propagandists. This modern tendency is seeking to determine the functions of physical education in a democracy and is striving constantly to be scientific and rational. Historically it has excellent models along certain lines, particularly in ancient Greek civilization, but its guide in America today is rather our social organization and the needs and capacities of men and women in a free form of government. . . . The calisthenics of Dio Lewis, the posturings of Catherine Beecher, the aesthetic dance of the Gilbert type with its formal poses and artificial movements are being replaced by a more wholesome, more educative, more artistic procedure.

In the foreword to another book on educational dance, Williams wrote: "it is worth believing . . . that the development of this kind of dancing sounds the death-knell of the acrobatic, ballet and aesthetic technic for educational institutions."[9]

Williams was rejecting the old physical education systems because they were not in line with modern education theory. But there was more to it than that. His disapproval of Europe and European gymnastic systems was part of a general American disillusionment and retreat into isolationism that followed World War I. The historian William E. Leuchtenburg has described this American attitude after the war: "Sounding the old theme of American innocence and European wickedness, the United States arraigned Europe as perversely war-loving, decadent, politically unorthodox and economically chaotic, and for welshing on its debts."[10] Whatever the reasons, what is especially significant about Williams's statements is that, for the first time, a leader outside the dance profession was encouraging America to develop its own unique dance art in line with its own unique views.

As we shall see, dance educators designed their systems in response to the needs of the new education. A few examples here will illustrate their specific adoption of Dewey's idea of education for democracy. Writing in 1925, Margaret H'Doubler asserted that the new form of dancing, which she and one or two others were developing, was "primarily democratic—as it must be if it is to fulfill its educational purposes in the public school curriculum." She had explained:

It serves all the ends of education—it helps to develop the body, to cultivate the love and appreciation of beauty, to stimulate the imagination and challenge the intellect, to deepen and refine the emotional life, and to broaden the social capacities of the individual that he may at once profit from and serve the greater world without. [11]

Strengthening social capacities was often mentioned by dance educators as one of the benefits of dance.

Preparation for democratic living persisted as an ideal in educational dance well beyond the 1920s. Writing in 1944, Ruth Radir, another dance educator, maintained that "Dance fulfills its function in the curricula of democracy's schools only if group work is so conducted that it is a little laboratory in democratic living." [12] Throughout *Modern Dance for the Youth of America*, she emphasized what she believed to be uniquely democratic about modern dance. In 1954, Alma Hawkins again detailed ways in which the college dance teacher can teach democratic principles and skills in her classroom. With its emergence into the modern education scene, dance in America was finally cosy with middle-class American ideals and values.

Spencer, Hall, Dewey, and their followers concentrated on how best to prepare a child for life as a social being—whether they interpreted that role as passive or active in relation to the environment. While they rejected nineteenth century authoritarian teaching methods, they did not at all reject the idea of discipline. They simply sought to instill self-discipline rather than obedience to outside discipline. While they recognized the need for self-expression and creative activity in the total education picture, this was just one of many concerns and not central to their programs.

In contrast to early progressive educators, one faction of postwar progressivism turned to self-expression and creativity as a way to cure society of its ills by curing the individual first. This group placed development of the individual as an individual at the center of their educational goals and methods. The idea was not self-discipline but freedom, self-knowledge, and self-expression.

The promoters of this point of view based their theories on an idealized concept of the artist and on Freud's psychoanalytic theory. At the end of World War I the idea of the artist as potential savior of a deranged America gained ground in some artistic, intellectual, and educational circles. The concept of the artist as a moral or spiritual leader was not new to America. As we have seen, it was introduced around the time of the revolution and again in the mid-nineteenth century. But the twentieth century version differed appreciably from those of the earlier periods. The late eighteenth century artist-philosopher was supposed to emphasize "ethical objectives, technical training, universal truth and sublime subject matter." The mid-nineteenth century artist-minister was to help "improve the nation's manners and morals," and to "promote virtue and oppose vice."[13] Both were called upon to support and promote established values.

The postwar years present a different picture. The artist now conceived of himself as outside society, free of its restrictions, in touch with a life and a truth unavailable within society. This was the heyday of expressionsim in American art. The center of the self-expression movement was Greenwich Village—"not only a place, a mood, a way of life," according to Malcolm Cowley, but "also a doctrine." The doctrine contained a number of ideas. Cowley summarized them as follows.

1. The idea of salvation by the child. . . . If . . . children are encouraged to develop their own personalities, to blossom freely like flowers, then the world will be saved by this new, free generation.
2. The idea of self-expression. . . .
3. The idea of paganism.—The body is a temple in which there is nothing unclean, a shrine to be adorned for the ritual of love.
4. The idea of living for the moment. . . .
5. The idea of liberty.—Every law, convention or rule of art that prevents self-expression or the full enjoyment of the moment should be shattered and abolished. Puritanism is the great enemy. . . .
6. The idea of female equality. . . .
7. The idea of psychological adjustment. . . .
8. The idea of changing place.—"They do things better in Europe."[14]

The high-priestess of this new religion was Isadora Duncan. She had said and done all these things. She lived her life as a shining example to the freedom seekers of the day.

The avant-garde artists and intellectuals believed that the artist offered the only hope of saving the world from the ill-effects of industrialization and rigidified civilization. As Floyd Dell had put it, the "real" world was so bad that the artist could exist in relation to it only by never growing up. The world, he said,

has made us choose between being children in a tiny sphere all our lives, or going into the larger world of reality as slaves. And I think we have made the right choice. For we have kept alive in our childish folly the flame of a sacred revolt against slavery. We have succeeded in making the world envious of our freedom. We have shown it the only way to be happy.[15]

Cremin notes that the staff of the short-lived but highly influential *Seven Arts* magazine (1916-1917) strongly denounced American culture and promoted "the intoxicating idea of artist-leaders who would unleash the true spiritual forces in American life." Where were the artist-leaders to come from? They would be created by the progressive schools. If every artist was a child, every child was an artist—until his creativity was stifled by outworn, repressive educational methods and the necessity of growing up a slave. The great task of education was to prepare the child for adulthood without destroying the artist in him. Cremin writes that the proponents of self-expression argued that "each individual has uniquely creative potentialities and that a school in which children are encouraged freely to develop these potentialities is the best guarantee of a larger society truly devoted to human worth and excellence." This faction had simply "expanded one part of what progressive education had formerly meant into its total meaning."[16]

Another major support for the self-expression approach came from Sigmund Freud's psychoanalytical theory. At the invitation of G. Stanley Hall in 1909, Freud had come to America and had delivered a series of lectures at Clark University. Slowly his ideas spread. Translations of his books appeared, and American scholars analyzed and discussed his theories. By the 1920s, educators working in the area of child-centered self-expression began to adopt his terminology and to apply his view of man. Teachers were encouraged to understand the Freudian concepts of repression, sublimation, transference, fixation, and the unconscious in terms of themselves and their students, and to be guided by these concepts in the classroom.

The artistic self-expressionists advocated creativity in the classroom so that the child might assert and express the positive aspects of his unique personality. Creative work was seen as both the result of freedom and a means to freedom. Educators wished to encourage the artist in the child because they believed the artist represented the higher nature of man. They wished to free the child from his repressed feelings because then his best nature—his artistic nature—would be able to assert itself. They believed in the perfectability of man by means of art and psychoanalytical techniques. And they believed in their own ability to manipulate the child to these ends.

This approach to education presented enormous problems. The ideal was students expressing in an orderly manner what their teachers thought they should, and becoming finer people as a result. The reality must have been chaos as individual selves in conflict went in unpredictable and anti-social directions. Cremin says of the self-expression movement:

Taken up as a fad, it elicited not only first-rate art, but every manner of shoddiness and self-deception as well. In too many classrooms license began to pass for liberty, planlessness for spontaneity, recalcitrance for individuality, obfuscation for art, and chaos for education—all justified in the rhetoric of expressionism.[17]

It was inevitable that after the initial enthusiasm the doctrine of self-expression became less extreme. Since education had to be accomplished in groups and had to prepare students for living in the real world, expressionism had to be brought within safe and reasonable bounds. It could not be allowed to interfere with a minimum of group order and had to be limited to what was socially acceptable.

Both the artistic and the Freudian sides of expressionsim have been prevalent in educational dance. Dance educators have often used the self-expression arguments to justify dance in the curriculum. But in practice, self-expression has to be curtailed for a number of reasons. Most teachers are neither psychotherapists nor artists, and their ability to lead in these directions is limited. If they happen to be trained in psychology or in professional dance, they will be inclined to stress one aspect of expression at the expense of the other. In addition, the time spent on dance in education is usually short, and the groups large. For these reasons there is little opportunity for totally free individual expression. The self-expression arguments offer a rationale for dance rather than a direction to be totally followed in practice.

Over and above these practical considerations, the theory of dance educators themselves militates against too free an expression. Without exception they are interested in shaping the kind of expression the student makes—for educational ends. The student is thus free to express only what the teacher considers valuable and worthwhile. Two examples will suffice to illustrate the point here.

H'Doubler has written that her philosophy of dancing is "based on a fundamental belief in the aesthetic capacities of man and the real worth of his expressing himself through creative activity, *if only he will express the best that is in him.*"[18] With beginning classes, H'Doubler would limit their freedom of choice even in the question of how a costume was designed, because she did not yet consider their taste developed enough to make a *right* choice. It is obvious throughout her work that H'Doubler advocates a disciplined training of skill and taste in dance education. What she and other dance educators taught was not really self-expression, but rather training in an expressionistic art form.

Hawkins, writing thirty years later, subscribed to similar ideas, but placed more stress on the therapeutic value of the dance experience. For example:

Dance offers a legitimate channel through which the individual can project his feelings—feelings of happiness, anxiety, or fear. Outlets which help the individual release tensions built up through emotional responses are a necessity if the organism is to function effectively and maintain good mental health.[19]

What if the student feels the urge to express hatred, viciousness, contempt? Such unacceptable feelings were never mentioned by dance educators, because they had not yet really investigated the relationship between dance activity and mental and emotional health. Only with the relatively recent emergence of dance therapy are such questions beginning to be explored.

This is not to belittle the value of dance in education. Undoubtedly, it is a wholesome activity that provides pleasure, physical exercise, some emotional release, and some art training even if it cannot hope to accomplish all that its promoters have claimed for it. The claims, however, have been useful in convincing educators and administrators that dance is a valuable activity for education. This has been all to the benefit of dance in America.

NOTES TO CHAPTER 6

1. *Education: Intellectual, Moral, and Physical,* p. 223.
2. Ibid., p. 281.
3. *The Transformation of the School,* p. 104.
4. *Educational Problems,* pp. 42-43.
5. Ibid., pp. 58-62.
6. *The Dewey School,* p. 260.
7. *The School and Society,* pp. 27-28.
8. Dewey and Dewey, *Schools of Tomorrow,* pp. 218-219.
9. Gertrude K. Colby, *Natural Rhythms and Dances,* p. 6.
10. *The Perils of Prosperity, 1914-32,* p. 105.
11. *Dance and Its Place in Education,* pp. 33, 35.
12. *Modern Dance for the Youth of America,* p. 4.
13. Neil Harris, *The Artist in American Society,* pp. 12, 300, 312.
14. *Exile's Return,* pp. 69-70.
15. *Were You Ever a Child?* pp. 121-122.
16. *The Transformation of the School,* pp. 202, 206.
17. Ibid., p. 207.
18. *Dance and Its Place in Education,* p. 7. [Italics mine.]
19. *Modern Dance in Higher Education,* p. 69.

Lucille Marsh, one of the early dance educators who contributed to the development of "natural dance." (Dance Collection, The New York Public Library at Lincoln Center.)

Margaret H'Doubler before 1926. Portrait by De Longe Studio, Madison, Wisconsin. (From State Historical Society of Wisconsin.)

Tableau of H'Doubler's students in a dance study from the 1920s. (From her *Dance and Its Place in Education*.)

The Crawl (backward). One of the exercises developed by Margaret H'Doubler for her classes at the University of Wisconsin. (From her *Dance and Its Place in Education*.)

CHAPTER 7

Diana, the Storm, and Cassim in the Cave: The New Dance in Higher Education

The framework for modern educational dance was developed at Teachers College, Columbia University by Gertrude Colby and her colleagues, and at the University of Wisconsin by Margaret H'Doubler. Both Colby and H'Doubler began their careers as instructors in physical education, became interested in dance around 1915, and by 1920 had established courses in dance in their respective departments. In these early years, senior physical education staff members felt the need to diversify their programs by including a creative dance activity, and they strongly encouraged Colby's and H'Doubler's experimentation.

The first to launch a modern educational dance course was Gertrude Colby. This was in 1913 at Speyer School, the demonstration school connected with Columbia University's Teachers College. After the Speyer School was dismantled in 1916, Colby became an instructor at Teachers College. It was here that she developed a course called "Natural Dance" for college women, which was offered under her direction from 1918 until 1931. During this lengthy career, Colby trained hundreds of dance teachers who carried the work to other schools throughout the country. Colby herself traveled to California in the summer of 1922 to teach natural dance at the University of California at Berkeley, remaining to teach at the Los Angeles campus of the university the following year.

Colby had received her initial physical education training at Dudley A. Sargent's school. Her dance training had included ballet with Louis Chalif, aesthetic dancing from Melvin Ballou Gilbert, and training in American Delsartism and Dalcroze eurythmics (see Appendix I). None of these systems seemed appropriate to the new goals of education that were in the air at Teachers College during the second decade of the new century.

Colby saw a need for "something less formal and more in harmony with the interests and activities of everyday life." So she set out to devise a new system. She experimented with elements from her varied training, but her ideas only crystallized after she saw Isadora Duncan dance. The naturalness and expressivity of Duncan's art approached the ideal of the progressive educators more than any other kind of theatrical dancing between 1910 and 1920.

In 1922 Colby published *Natural Rhythms and Dances,* which is primarily a collection of studies and dances to be used by the teacher. In the introduction, Colby briefly described the typical 1920s progressive interest in the child as the source of art, beauty, spontaneity, and naturalness. She based her approach on familiar movements—walking, skipping, running, leaping, playing ball, rolling hoops, flying kites—because she considered these the natural rhythms of childhood. Natural dancing was simply a training "to preserve the natural spontaneity of the child while developing depth and maturity of expression and experience." With enthusiasm and optimism, Colby was sure that "by starting with something known . . . we gain confidence and satisfaction in our dancing, lose self-consciousness . . . and build, and build again until we have attained something far above the thing from which we started."[1]

But Colby was not particularly enthusiastic about the concept of self-expression—or rather, she stressed the second part of it rather than the first. From a psychological point of view, she maintained, a dance could be self-expressive only if the dancer expressed "in spontaneous rhythm an emotion spontaneously felt." That, she believed, occurred rarely, and never within group work. She was apparently not interested in stimulating that kind of self-expression, for she had students develop their dances from external rather than internal stimuli. She admitted, though, that once an idea or emotional theme was chosen for a dance, it would become "a part of the individual and the resulting expression [would be] her own."

Music played a major role in Colby's new system. It was used for all the natural dances, but some of the dances were based on music alone, without any other theme or idea brought in. Colby shows here her Dalcroze influence. She justified this kind of dance as education in music appreciation; and in working with music she stressed understanding of the structural organization of a piece, having the student study its "phrases, accents, climaxes, and mood as well as rhythm."

In opposition to earlier varieties of educational dance, such as aesthetic or gymnastic dance, Colby placed little emphasis on technique. She considered it to be the means to the end of expression and believed it should not be developed until there was a need for it. "When ideals outgrow the power to express," she wrote, "then desire for a more responsive body is felt and the time for technic is ripe." The only general principle of technique she conceived was "along the line of natural movements with the purpose of developing a greater freedom, a better poise and control—in a word, to make the body better as an instrument of expression." This statement could have been taken straight out of a Delsartian manual. Colby did apply an esthetic standard to the work, and what she chose was characteristically Delsartian and Duncan-inspired as well. Her standard, she said, was "based upon art, especially as found in Greek sculpture and vases; upon the laws of line and mass, of balance and of opposition."

What Colby considered depth and maturity of expression is illustrated by the fourteen natural dances she presents with descriptions and music in her book. These were presumably designed for college women and include *The Frolic, The Faun, Huntresses,* and *Chariot of Apollo.* They are set to music by composers such as Schubert, Grieg, Chopin, Beethoven, Tchaikovsky, and Delibes.

Some of the dances are no more than musical interpretations, but most have at least the suggestion of a story that is expressed through natural movements. An example of a solo dance is *The Last Rose,* in which

A lovely rose blooms late in the autumn, long after the time of roses. As the last petal unfolds, she gazes up enraptured at the blue sky and the sun above her.

She looks around the garden for others of her own kind and is disappointed to find she is alone. But the world seems so beautiful that she dances happily in the breeze, despite her loneliness.

Suddenly she sees a storm cloud. She is frightened but tries to forget it in dancing. A cold wind blows upon her and she realizes that she also must depart to join the summer roses.

"Oh why must I leave this beautiful world? I have only started to live when I must die!"[2]

A perfect Delsartian exercise!

Colby's dance themes are removed from the here-and-now of the dancer and placed in a classical Greek setting or in the world of nature. Her group dances are built around stories of Greek gods or huntresses or youths frolicking in the summertime, with girls taking the male parts.

Colby's themes may not appear deep and mature today—or related to everyday life. But in the 1920s they were significantly new in educational dance. The interest in expressing any kind of theme contrasted sharply with the brute force of gymnastic dancing and the pretty posing of aesthetic dance. In addition, an interest in Greek culture and in nature indicated a commitment to then popular styles of art and beauty—a new element in physical education. The new dance considered its neo-classic themes advanced, whereas such themes were deemed old-fashioned and reactionary in painting and sculpture. But Colby's decision to work for the expression of ideas in dance—however naive the results—was an attempt to bring dance up to date in the context of the other arts.

Ruth Murray, who studied with Colby at Columbia from 1923 to 1925, remembers her as a teacher who was "always encouraging, enthusiastic, and interested in the creative talents of her students." And the students of those years—whether their interest was in dance or in athletics—flocked to her classes. Murray performed in two of the dance recitals directed by Colby and has described how Colby collaborated with the students in the creation of dances for production. She writes:

While the subject, the music, and the general spatial and movement design of my dance was pre-determined, I was given the responsibility for working out the actual movement sequence which composed the total "flow." As I recall now, she was a liberal critic and made only a few changes in my conception of the whole. Also, some of the group dances in which I participated were partially choreographed by the dancers themselves.[3]

Colby synthesized various trends in education and in dance that had appeared in the late nineteenth and early twentieth centuries. By combining ideas from Delsartism, Dalcroze, and Duncan with progressive education theories she created an educational dance form that satisfied the needs of physical education departments. She introduced her system on both the east and west coasts. Dance in higher education was launched in a direction that it would continue to follow in some respects up to the present day.

To Jesse Feiring Williams, the chairman of the Physical Training Department at Teachers College, the significance of Colby's work went far beyond mere physical fitness goals. In the foreword to *Natural Rhythms and Dances* he wrote:

Modern man has builded great cities, he has erected economic standards of success, he has transformed the world industrially and has forced himself into a life of sedentary toil. When he looks at the result of his work he finds it is not good. . . . In combating the handicaps and hazards of modern life, it has not always been clear that the way lay in the restoration of the desirable elements in nature. Physical Education will make its contribution in modern times, not by proposing artificialities . . . but rather by emphasizing the essential needs of man and by offering natural forms that represent the best motor expression of the human race. . . . Natural Rhythms and Dances is symbolic of a new spirit in physical education.

Again and again this thought is expressed in the writings of the progressive educators—that man is in trouble because he has severed his ties with nature. And just as often, the cure is seen in natural, creative, expressive activity.

Two years after the publication of Colby's *Natural Rhythms and Dances,* Jesse Feiring Williams introduced another book on the same subject written by Agnes L. Marsh of Teachers College and Lucile Marsh of Smith College. Their work, *The Dance in Education*, is also a teacher's manual with model lesson plans, studies and dances, music, and directions on teaching methods. The Marshes had systematized and elaborated natural dancing, and their work represents a more mature development of the form.

The Marshes never mentioned self-expression. Their desire was to teach dancing as "a great art, full of educational opportunities, and rich in inspiration for art and life." They did have the typical progressive faith in the artist as the best of human beings, and their attitude toward technique paralleled Colby's exactly. The natural movements they listed as the basis of their work were walking, running, skipping, leaping, whirling, galloping, stretching, bending, jumping, throwing, grasping, turning, and relaxation.

As the Marshes explained their educational theory, it derived from Spencer and Dewey more than from the expressionistic school. They wrote that education must "meet the needs of everyday life," and they recognized three parts to education: the physical, the mental, and the moral. They believed that dancing, if it was to be "a great instrument of education," must (1) aid and maintain bodily growth and development, (2) interest the student and offer stimulus to the full extent of his maturity, and (3) further social adjustment.

In their view, dance contributes to the first of these requirements by instilling good postural habits and physical efficiency in all the natural movements of the system. It could fulfill the second if the study of dance was linked to all the other subjects in the curriculum—art, music, history, religion, philosophy, psychology, and so on. Actually, the Marshes' book provides specific material for accomplishing this goal, correlating each study or dance with one or more of the arts and with other fields of study.

The Marshes considered their third requirement of education (social adjustment) fulfilled by dance since, as they taught it, dance entailed a great deal of cooperation among students and between students and faculty. Furthermore, they argued, "the necessary informality of creative work of this kind enables the teacher to observe and develop the personalities of his students and their relations to one another."

One can see in the Marshes' presentation elements of American Delsartism, Dalcroze, Duncan, and Denishawn. Their heavy emphasis on Greek culture as a source, their use of Greek statues as models for poses and movements, and their whole approach to expression is Delsartian. Dalcroze provided them with a theoretical understanding of the relationship of movement to the understanding of music. They agreed with Duncan and the Delsartians when they insisted that every movement must be motivated. For example, they wrote, "if we want a joyous skip, the first thing we must do is find the motivation and then skip and continue to skip to this idea until we have perfected the movement." They were careful to motivate even their preliminary exercises in rotation, relaxation, walking, and running.

The Marshes used much of the same music that Duncan favored— the composers Wagner, Beethoven, Chopin, Mendelssohn, Tchaikovsky, and others. It is not surprising that they also often chose similar subject matter. The most striking parallel is in their *Marche Slav*, which bears the stamp of the Duncan interpretation as described by Carl Van Vechten.

The last section of the book is devoted to an Egyptian dance drama entitled *Isis*, which appears to be a direct steal from Denishawn. This is not the only element representing that company's work. For years, Ruth St. Denis, Ted Shawn, and their company had been popularizing Greek impressions, nature dances, and music visualizations as well as the more elaborate exotic productions. Their influence can be felt throughout the book.

From their choice of subject matter for dance, it would seem that the Marshes had studied and followed Hall's recommendations on educational dance as well as the Denishawn format. For example, they based dances on elements of nature—night, dawn, a storm, snowflakes, waves, trees—and on themes from mythology and history featuring Greek gods, warriors, hunters, revelries, and festivals. For humor they included a dance of Pierrot and Pierrette; for tragedy a dance of Cassim, an Arabian Nights character who seeks treasure in a cave and is trapped.

The Marshes focused on the grotesque and sinister with a marionette's funeral march and with a dance of bats. They made up two dances about American Indians. They based dances on themes like rumor, happiness, and human liberation. Seven out of the fifteen full-scale dances have something to do with death or killing. Romanticized as these are, they represent an early attempt to link dance with real human experience. As Hall advocated, they attempt to touch every aspect of human life and culture. The Marshes, like Colby, did not deal with any of their themes in a contemporary realistic setting. But this is no surprise. In 1924 Ted Shawn, who would pioneer in the use of contemporary American themes, was just getting started in that vein.

The work of Colby, the Marshes, and other teachers of natural dancing furnished a transition between old and new approaches to dance in education—just as the work of Duncan, St. Denis, and Shawn served as a transition in professional dance.

The most important center for the continuing development of the new and progressive in educational dance was at the University of Wisconsin under the direction of Margaret H'Doubler. The work of this pioneer has had a much more lasting influence than that of any of the other early dance educators. H'Doubler developed a sophisticated and detailed system and philosophy of educational dance based on scientific principles. She wrote extensively on the subject, and her books are still used in educational dance classes. Finally, she continued teaching at Wisconsin until the 1960s—which means that she was training students on a regular basis for over forty years. Even after she retired, H'Doubler continued to spread her philosophy, knowledge, and inspiration in guest teaching engagements, and the hundreds of students who trained with her are passing the approach on to new generations of dancers. It is to be expected that in a career of such length, ideas would be modified, insights deepened, and methods developed and refined.

Like Colby, H'Doubler started her career in physical education. The head of her department at Wisconsin, Blanche Trilling, recognized the need for dance in the program and asked H'Doubler to investigate the possibilities. In 1916, at Trilling's request, H'Doubler spent a year in New York doing graduate work at Teachers College, studying movement with the music teacher Alys Bentley, attending performances of Diaghilev's Ballets Russes and of Isadora Duncan, and discussing dance with Colby and with Bird Larson (another educational dance innovator whose influence was cut short by her early death in 1927).

Returning to Wisconsin in 1917, H'Doubler began to work on a system of dance for use in physical education classes. This system was eventually incorporated into the university curriculum, and word of her classes soon spread to other institutions. Colleges and universities began to request a teacher-training program so that they too could offer this new dance in their physical education programs. In 1926 Wisconsin initiated the first teacher-training courses, and a year later it established the first dance major to be offered in an institution of higher education.

Happily, H'Doubler has written extensively on her philosophy of education and dance. In 1921 she published *A Manual of Dancing;* in 1925, *Dance and Its Place in Education*.

Her bibliography reveals H'Doubler as a well-educated woman who had read widely in many areas. Besides an extensive knowledge of dance literature, she was familiar with a wide spectrum of works on education, esthetics, physiology, psychology, anthropology, evolutionary theory, religion, art history, philosophy, mythology, and music. Among her mentors she included the progressive education theorists Hall, Dewey, and Thorndike; three authors who had at least some connection with nineteenth century expression and probably with Delsartism; and Dalcroze's writings. That H'Doubler did a great deal of reasearch in the development of her approach is obvious in her writings. She brought to educational dance a breadth of vision comparable to what Duncan brought to theatrical dance.

H'Doubler's theoretical discussion of dance and its place in education reveals her commitment to the ideas and goals of the progressive educators. We have seen that she reflected Dewey's concept of education for democracy. There is also much of G. Stanley Hall in her thought, even though she believed in education as a means of reforming life rather than merely adapting to a fixed world.

H'Doubler accepted Hall's evolutionary concepts and saw the history of dance in those terms. After giving a résumé of the historical development of dance from a lower to a higher form, H'Doubler proposed that

in order to evolve the dance as an art in the individual it should be developed along the lines of its racial evolution. At first . . . it was crude, instinctive and expressive of exuberant life. Gradually, by laws of his own nature, man learned to master the working material of his medium, and was led on to higher planes of conscious expression.[4]

She thus advocated a dance training progression that would recapitulate the "racial history" of the dance. Interestingly, the training approaches described in her books do not sound as though they do that at all.

H'Doubler reflected both Hall's thinking and the self-expression doctrine when she advocated exercising the emotions by expressing them through dance.

The average person tends to be constrained and awkward, and in certain parts of America, largely because of the Puritan tradition, exceedingly reserved. Often his feelings are so effectually repressed that they become thin and barren.[5]

She pointed out that emotional expression was essential for psychological health, but saw no panacea in dance. She denied that the imaginative rendition of an emotion could provide relief for deeply rooted emotional problems. What she did say was that dancing, like "any form of free and joyous self-expression, eases tension and opens the way for the free expression of other emotions."

H'Doubler also had much to say about artistic creativity. Basing her argument on her wide knowledge of esthetics, psychology, and art history, she tied the artistic impulse to the physiological and psychological nature of man. Art, she wrote, arises out of the "instinct to express all feeling in order to continue pleasurable states of feeling, and to obtain relief from that which is not pleasurable." Back of all art manifestations, she found "one fundamental impulse . . . the craving for self-expression," or, put another way, man's need "to realize his dream of life in some form outside of himself."[6] H'Doubler did not make extravagant claims for self-expression as a cure for society's problems. She simply considered it central to life rather than peripheral. And it follows that as a need, art has a decided place in education.

In contrast to Colby, H'Doubler was committed to the idea of self-expression in the interest of both creativity and psychological well-being. But she advocated no indulgent, anarchic expression. She defined the art of dancing as "self-expression through the medium of bodily movement; a revealing of mental and emotional states, stimulated and regulated, or both, usually by music."[7] If she were asked whether she would consider joyous running and leaping to be dance—if it were stimulated by the wind, for example—she would say no, because she believed that it was the

systematizing according to the laws of the medium that separates art from accident and nature. It is only when these random, yet expressive movements are subjected to the harmonizing influence of rhythm, or time sequence that the dance proper comes into being.[8]

The art of dance of H'Doubler, then, involved organized self-expression.

In sharper contrast to Colby, H'Doubler considered technique a necessary preliminary to dancing because it created flexibility, control, and strength in the body. In addition, her fundamental exercises were designed to provide an understanding of how the body functions and what movements are possible to it and healthful for it. These exercises consisted of

a series of movements which in themselves demand fundamental coordinations, most of them beginning in the spine and extending in a well-ordered progression to all the smaller muscle groups of the extremities. Because of the muscular activity involved in the upright position, many of the fundamentals are executed lying on the floor, thus relieving the body of the pull of gravity.[9]

Since an understanding of the body's functioning is basic in H'Doubler's approach, she insisted that a teacher must know enough physics, anatomy, and kinesiology to give the students an adequate conception of what they were doing. H'Doubler herself, as an undergraduate, was a biology major with physics and chemistry minors.

H'Doubler's early method contained exercises for every major part of the body, going from simple to complex in every case. She too used the word *natural* to describe her approach. It *is* natural in the sense that it is based on contemporary scientific knowledge about what is healthy for human beings, but it is *not* natural in the sense that it lacks an acquired technique. A dancer who has mastered all of H'Doubler's preliminary exercises would have a much larger vocabulary of movement than would either an untrained person or a student trained in Colby's natural dancing, in Delsartism, or in Duncan's style of dance.

H'Doubler's method as described in her early books most resembles that of Dalcroze in its thoroughness, in its attention to the quality and varying body-tensions in movement, and in its emphasis on understanding what is happening in the body during the execution of a movement. Furthermore, both systems are natural in the sense that they do not impose arbitrary mannerisms but instead try to discover each students potential abilities. These are then developed along lines that are healthful to the body until a technical mastery is achieved.

In addition to technique, H'Doubler considered some degree of musical understanding necessary for dancing. Although she realized that it was possible to dance without music, she preferred using it because, she wrote, "there is such a special and organic relationship between the two arts, and so much to be gained from building on that relationship, that the teacher of dance will want to open its resources to her students."[10]

She recommended that the teacher first explain the structure of music, then have the students practice simple locomotion to various rhythms, and finally work up to the dynamic interpretation of entire pieces. This process, she felt, should take at least a semester. Afterward, the students would be ready to work on true dances.

What kind of dances resulted from H'Doubler's approach? In *Dance And Its Place in Education* she described the dances presented by a group of her students in 1924. A few of the dances sound similar to natural dances—Apollo with the horses of the sun, for example, and a bacchanale. But in general the themes are drawn from broader sources and treated with greater subtlety. There are few Greek themes and no serious interpretations of plants, animals, or natural elements. The only animals depicted are comic figures.

The program is almost equally divided among lyrical, dramatic, and comic dances. The lyrical dances are primarily music interpretations. The dramatic dances tell of such things as Arachne, a goddess fated to turn into a spider; Volga boatmen struggling with their boat; and the rendezvous of a shepherd and shepherdess. Most of the comic dances are based on children's stories or nursery rhymes. Last on the program is a tragicomic dance drama with several scenes and a large cast.

Each of the dances required a particular aspect of technical proficiency for its execution. In *Raggedy Ann and Andy*, for example, the dancers had to create the effect of being dolls without skeletal structures—and thus with great equilibrium problems. *Tarentella* presented another kind of difficulty. In that dance,

a peasant girl, stung by the venom of a tarantula, summons her companions. imploring them to dance with her to drive the fearful poison from her veins. . . . Arms interlaced, the three leap forward, backward, circling in and out, spinning and swirling in a desperate combat with the tightening snare of death. Exhausted, first one companion, then the other falls, rising in pain to battle still for the luckless maiden.

H'Doubler points out the difficulty of control in this dance. While the upper body gave the illusion of fatigue, the legs and feet had to continue moving faster and faster. Such things could not have been done without a well-developed technique.

The themes and dances described by H'Doubler represent a significant advance over those found in the natural dance manuals. She is not limited to the romantic and neoclassic clichés that were becoming out of date by the 1920s. In addition, her dances appear to have been more demanding technically and more sophisticated in their treatment of form and content. Artistically, too, they were probably more satisfying than the natural dances of Colby and the Marshes. There can be no doubt about where H'Doubler stood on the question of artistic standards as against educational goals. She would never have sacrificed the one for the other. Nevertheless, her system was rigorous and demanding—not at the expense of educational goals, but in the interest of them.

There is an underlying aspect of H'Doubler's thought that is typical of progressive thought in general and that shaped progressive education programs long after progressivism as a political force was dead. This was her tremendous optimism and self-confidence. The progressives were dissatisfied with their world. They saw industrialization, technology, materialism, and corruption as running rampant, intruding on man's contact with nature, his spontaneity, his higher self, and his happiness. But they believed fervently in the perfectability of man and society—and in the omnipotence of science. They had no doubt that a scentificially designed educational program could better the individual and thus better the world. And they were convinced that educators could find out all there was to know about human needs and how to satisfy them.

This optimism permeated H'Doubler's work. After enumerating the failures of modern civilization and traditional education, she stated that education was encouraging individual development. But that very encouragement, she believed, was creating further demands for educational reform. Society had to free the individual to go after what *he* wanted. It also had to shape his desires in the interest of human and social well-being. It had to

give him adequate acquaintance with the various planes of desirable things that he may learn to discriminate and to elect the higher rather than the lower. . . . For the aim of education, as Henmon has aptly defined it, is "To bring an individual from where he is to where he ought to be."[11]

Jesse Feiring Williams put it this way:

The satisfaction of human wants is the most important business of the world when judged by the activity of men and women everywhere. Contrariwise, the education and training of people to want that which is good is infinitely more worth while.[12]

These educators were confident that there was an absolute good— that the youth of the nation had to be educated to recognize it and choose it. They created educational programs that they hoped would do this, and they believed that this would make the world a finer place.

That Margaret H'Doubler has more than fulfilled her goals as a teacher is enthusiastically verified by her students. Mary Jane Wolber, a dance educator who studied with H'Doubler in the 1940s has written: "her good humor and warm affection endeared her to us all. It is difficult to imagine what dance education would be like in the U.S. had it not been for the vision and zeal of this beautiful woman."[13] Lonny Joseph Gordon, who studied with H'Doubler in the 1960s:

Her electric energy was immediate and her ideas very clear. . . . She had us moving in no time flat and not until two hours had passed and she thanked us for being so eager . . . did we realize all we had experienced. There was great joy in her classes—we laughed with her quick wit. She made "learning" so enjoyable and clear that everyone was captivated.[14]

And Anna Halprin, who perhaps more than anyone else has realized for a later generation of dancers the ideals and vision pioneered by H'Doubler, remembers studying with her, beginning in 1938:

Above all else, Marge wanted to be for others a vehicle to transmit knowledge, the kind of knowledge that was impeccably true; knowledge that was objective and thus beyond her own personal claim. She was humble in a beautiful, strong, clear way. This attitude made the process of receiving an education from her totally your own responsibility. . . . I found her egoless and dedicated to her role as a giver of knowledge that she firmly believed in. . . . She was not a dancer per se, she did not teach by teaching a style of movement. Her teaching method was through charts, scribbles on the blackboard and being a catalyst that guided you through a creative process. I was always stimulated by her incredible grasp of her materials, her delightful appreciation of all of us responding in our own movement, her ever present sense of joy and vitality which in itself was a model.[15]

Margaret H'Doubler continues, in her eighties, to have the same keen interest in dancers, dancing, and dance education, and she continues to stimulate, challenge, and inspire all those whose lives touch hers.

Colby, H'Doubler, and their followers initiated a variety of educational dance that differed from the earlier forms in both theory and practice. Their goals, standards, and teaching methods were drawn from contemporary progressive theory and rejected the old, outworn formulas for art and education. But their work differed from earlier physical education systems in yet another way. These innovators conceived of their new educational dance as a form of theatrical dancing, albeit on an amateur level. The educational dance and quasi-dance gymnastics of the eighteenth and nineteenth centuries were not at all designed for presentation in theatrical settings. They were done for pleasure, cultivation, physical exercise.

In contrast, the dances described by Colby, the Marshes, and H'Doubler are theater pieces. They are expressions—whether of the self or of something else. And an expression, notwithstanding Hall's disclaimer, implies an audience. But more than this, they are specifically designed for performance. It is significant that H'Doubler included a discussion of public performance in her text, as would subsequent writers on educational dance.

The pioneers in dance education clearly articulated a beginning philosophy of dance for the American scene. They synthesized the ideals and practical work of Duncan and Denishawn with the ideas of modern American philosophers and educators. They brought theatrical dance into the American university as a medium for expressing American aspirations. The uses of dance for education and the value of educational dance products in terms of the standards of professional dance would come into question in subsequent years. But it cannot be denied that the incorporation of the art into education gave dance a respectable base in America and provided it with the institutional and financial support that kept it alive and allowed it to grow.

NOTES TO CHAPTER 7

1. Colby, *Natural Rhythms and Dances,* pp. 7-9.
2. Ibid., p. 85.
3. Letter to the author, April 3, 1975.
4. *Dance and Its Place in Education,* pp. 28-29.
5. Ibid., p. 223.
6. Ibid., pp. 12, 13-14.
7. *Manual of Dancing,* p. 7.
8. *Dance and Its Place in Education,* p. 15.
9. *Manual of Dancing,* p. 8.
10. *Dance and Its Place in Education,* p. 147.
11. Ibid., pp. 5-6.
12. Colby, *Natural Rhythms and Dances,* p. 5.
13. Letter to the author, May 22, 1975.
14. Letter to the author, May 30, 1975.
15. Letter to the author, April 6, 1975.

CHAPTER 8

In Conclusion

By 1930, dance as a serious art form had gained a precarious foothold in American culture. The number of dance concerts in New York City increased spectacularly during the late 1920s and the 1930s despite the depression and the poverty of the dancers. In addition to performances of ballet, the Duncan and Denishawn styles, and Spanish dance, more and more concerts featured modern dance, the next stage in the development of an anti-formalistic tradition in American dance.

The most prominent innovators and leaders of modern dance were Martha Graham, Doris Humphrey, and Charles Weidman—all of whom were trained in the Denishawn school. They, their colleagues from other traditions, and their students created a wealth of dance activity in the 1930s, a decade in which America's potential for vital and significant dance production became evident. Modern dancers questioned the established approaches to dance and devoted their energies to portraying movements and forms that would reflect the life of their day. They were concerned with reality, contemporaneity, and relevance to the social, political, and psychological problems they saw around them.

Audiences were small and funds meager. Nevertheless, the number of concerts as well as the numbers of performers, students, dance groups, and knowledgeable and interested spectators continued to grow. Beginning in the 1930s people throughout the United States could become acquainted with modern dance as professional companies began to tour and as performing college dance groups began to proliferate. Modern dance was subjected to ridicule, particularly in the hinterlands, but enough people became interested to keep the art alive and developing.

There was close collaboration between dance in higher education and professional modern dance. The professionals depended on the universities for teaching stints and performing engagements; they could hardly have continued their work without such support. In turn, university dance educators greatly valued the professional dancers for their skills and their artistry as well as for the stimulus they offered the students—although there has always been the question of whether the goals and the consequent teaching methods should be the same for both educational and professional dance training.

The trend begun in the late 1920s has continued and intensified up to the present day. Universities and colleges are still the most important patrons of modern dance. They still provide the most work for teachers and performers, train the most students, and sponsor the most performances. Although modern dance is offered under other auspices at times, its dependence on academic support is considerable.

Other American institutions that have supported dance since the 1930s have been government agencies and private foundations. Small but significant dance projects were funded by the federal government under the Works Progress Administration in the late 1930s. There has been some state and city government sponsorship of the arts from which dance has benefited slightly. The State Department has sent American dance companies abroad to represent American culture. And most recently, support for dance companies and choreography has come from the National Endowment for the Arts. Private foundations have long contributed to the development of American ballet, but their support of modern dance has been increasing in recent years.

It does not matter what kind of American dance is receiving the most support. What *does* matter is that dance as an art form is now valued and respected to the extent that established American institutions are behind it rather than indifferent or hostile.

All this is not to say that American dance has economic strength or that it enjoys the support it deserves. On the contrary, a continuing theme from the 1930s to the present day is economic weakness. But dance has come a long way since the beginning of the twentieth century. There is an entity that can be recognized as America's contribution to the art of dance, and it has a superb international reputation.

The American dance world today has variety, richness, and brilliance, including not only modern dance and its offshoots, but also a revitalized ballet tradition (influenced by developments in modern dance) and various ethnic dance forms. Dance is supported by educational, governmental, and private organizations. Audiences are at an all-time high, and dancers and choreographers have a respected place in American society.

Dance has arrived. It has in fact developed beyond the wildest imaginings of the reformers and visionaries who dared to believe that an American dance art was possible.

APPENDIXES

APPENDIX I

Dalcroze Eurythmics

Emile Jaques-Dalcroze was a French music teacher who had studied under Delibes in Paris and Bruckner in Vienna before becoming professor of harmony in Geneva in 1892. Disturbed that music education was mechanical and ineffectual in the nineteenth century's last years, he devised a system of music training that involved rhythmic body exercises to intensify the appreciation and understanding of musical rhythms. The system was based on his belief that a connection existed between rhythm in hearing or creating harmonies and rhythm as experienced in moving.

Dalcroze's experiments led him into other areas besides music. In his *Rhythm, Music and Education*, a collection of essays written from 1898 to 1919, he discusses education, theater, and dancing as well. *Eurythmics, Art and Education,* a collection of later essays, treats of rhythm and music in relation to the cinema, the lyric theater, education, art, criticism, the blind, and dance. A few chapters are devoted to a complete system he had devised for teaching a new kind of dance that he hoped would replace the forms he considered sterile and decadent.

To Dalcroze, dancing was "the art of expressing emotions by means of rhythmic bodily movements." He felt that rhythm could control and refine emotions, thus removing them from the particular and subjective into the realm of art. He criticized ballet as "an exaggerated development of bodily virtuosity at the expense of expression." Furthermore, in ballet the various parts of the body did not harmonize with each other, in his opinion, nor did the body as a whole relate to the music. He attributed this in part to the great separation between the training of dancers and the training of musicians. Dancers knew nothing of music except metronomic counting; composers did not understand how the body moves or what it is capable of doing.

To remedy the situation, Dalcroze recommended special training that began with simple walking, without arm movements, on a flat surface in strict time to music ranging from the very fast to the very slow. When this was mastered, the student practiced walking rhythmically on stairs of various heights and on inclines strewn with objects. Arm movements were studied separately at first—to discover the many nuances possible in the language of gesture.

By 1905 Dalcroze had evolved a system for dancing which he called "moving plastic." Believing that dance must have continuity, that the transitions between positions were more important than the poses themselves, he created exercises that would develop the skill of moving continuously. This was in response, so he said, to the tendency of ballet and Greek dancers to assume one decorative pose after another without paying attention to the movement in between.

Struck by the stiffness of the usual gymnastic movements, I conceived *continuous bodily movements,* analogous to those of the bow on the string or a sustained sound on a wind instrument. The slowness of these continuous movements is the product of muscular resistance. I caused them to first be practiced separately and then connected them with arrested movements in order, finally, to have them executed in conjunction with these latter (polyrhythm).[1]

He devised such movements for the various parts of the body while standing in one place, or for the whole body while it was moving in space—either from low to high in place, or horizontally across the floor. All these movements are illustrated in the book.

Certain studies Dalcroze considered indispensable if continuity was to be mastered. These included passing from a state of total relaxation, lying on the floor, to various stages of raising the body erect; the effects of breathing on the spatial and dynamic movements of different parts of the body; various speeds and dynamics in locomotion; the effects of yielding to or resisting weight; and the varying degrees of energy and duration in all movements. Lying on the floor for exercises was an innovation that would be used extensively by modern dancers. Rather than a vocabulary of specific steps such as is taught in ballet, Dalcroze aimed at teaching a vocabulary of movement qualities.

Dalcroze's system gained considerable recognition. In 1910, he built a school near Dresden. Within three years it had more than 600 students, both children and adults, from sixteen countries. His influence reached such European dancers as Nijinsky, Marie Rambert, Mary Wigman, and Hanya Holm.

Dalcroze's system was taught at Denishawn and provided part of the background training for both Colby and H'Doubler. Its influence was pervasive. One teacher of the 1920s, Elsa Findlay, had studied with Dalcroze for years at the Hellerau school. She came to the United States after World War I and taught eurythmics at Columbia University, at Vassar, at Boleslavsky's and Ouspenskaya's Laboratory Theater, and elsewhere. Translations of Dalcroze's writings began to appear in this country in 1921. In 1926 Paul Boepple, who had been Dalcroze's chief assistant at the Geneva Dalcroze Institute since 1919, was sent to New York to assume directorship over a New York Dalcroze School of Music.

Dalcroze's philosophy of education was strikingly similar to that of the progressive educators in America.

The object of education is to enable pupils to say at the end of their studies, not "I know," but "I experience," and then to create the desire of *self-expression*. For when we experience an emotion strongly, we feel the need to pass it on to others to the utmost of our power. The more life we have, the more we shall be able to give to others. To receive and to give: such is the great rule for all mankind. . . .

A true teacher should be both psychologist, physiologist, and artist. When a pupil leaves a school, he should be capable not only of living normally but also of feeling life with a certain emotion. . . . It is important that education should devote like attention to intellectual and to physical development.[2]

The Dalcroze system was appropriate to the progressive era in America. Not only did it parallel philosophically the trends in education; it also furnished a well-thought-out and detailed method of physical and artistic training in which both body and mind took part. The respect it continued to receive in educational dance circles is attested to by the inclusion of a section on it in Frederick Rand Rogers's giant compilation, *Dance: A Basic Educational Technique* of 1941.

NOTES TO APPENDIX I

1. Emile Jaques-Dalcroze, *Eurythmics, Art and Education*, pp. 66-67.
2. Ibid., pp. 58-59.

APPENDIX II

A Tentative List
of Delsartian Books in English
in Chronological Order

This list has been compiled from the Library of Congress Catalogue, the British Museum Catalogue, and references in the works on Delsartism cited in the bibliography that follows.

1882
Delaumosne, Abbé. *The Art of Oratory, System of Delsarte.* Translated from the French by Frances A. Shaw, Albany, N.Y.: E. S. Werner.

1884
Foster, Joe E. *The Philosophy of Elocution.* London: Simpkin and Marshall.

1885
Foster, Joe E. *The Art of Expression.* A book for clergymen, barristers, vocalists, actors, etc. London: Simpkin and Marshall.
Stebbins, Genevieve. *The Delsarte System of Expression.* New York: Edgar S. Werner.

1886
Brown, Moses True. *The Synthetic Philosophy of Expression.* As applied to the arts of reading, oratory and personation. Boston: Houghton Mifflin.
Foster Joe E. *The Art of Preaching.* London: Simpkin and Marshall.
Stebbins, Genevieve. *The Delsarte System of Expression.* New York: E. S. Werner.
Stebbins, Genevieve. *The Delsarte System of Dramatic Expression.* New York: E. S. Werner.
Either of the above two listings, or both, may refer to the Stebbins

1885 edition—or perhaps to a later printing of it. The first citation comes from the British Museum Catalogue; the second from the Library of Congress Catalogue.

1887

The Delsarte System of Oratory. 3d ed. New York: E. S. Werner.

Stebbins, Genevieve. *The Delsarte System of Expression.* 2d ed. New York: E. S. Werner.

1888

Stebbins, Genevieve. *Society Gymnastics.* Referred to in the Wilbor Addendum to the 1902 edition of Stebbins, *The Delsarte System of Expression.*

1889

Morgan, Anna. *An Hour with Delsarte; A Study of Expression.* Boston: Lee and Shepard.

Wilbor, Elsie M., comp. *Delsarte Recitation Book.* New York: E. S. Werner.

1890

Sanburn, Frederic, comp. *A Delsartean Scrap-book; Health, Personality, Beauty, House Decoration, etc.* With Preface by Walter Crane. 11th ed. New York: Lovell, Gestefeld. No. 124 of Lovell's Literature Series.

Wilbor, Elsie M., ed. *Delsarte Recitation Book and Directory.* New York: E. S. Werner.

1891

Le Favre, Mrs. Caroline (Carrica) Williams. *Delsartean Physical Culture; With Principles of the Universal Formula.* New York: Fowler and Wells.

Sanburn, Frederick. *A Delsartean Scrap-book . . .* New York: U.S. Book Co. See listing under 1890.

1892

Bishop, Emily M. *Americanized Delsarte Culture.* Meadville, Pa.: Flood and Vincent; Chautauqua-Century Press. The British Museum Catalog says this was published in Washington by the author.

Le Favre, Carrica (Mrs. Caroline Williams). *Physical Culture, Founded on Delsartean Principles.* New York: Fowler and Wells. No. 7 of The Science of Health Library.

Warman, Edward B. *Gestures and Attitudes: An Exposition of the Delsarte Philosophy of Expression.* Boston: Lee and Shepard.

1893

Delsarte System of Oratory, 4th ed. New York: E. S. Werner. Includes writings of Delaumosne, Arnaud, Delsarte, Geraldy, Giraudet, Durivage, and Berlioz.

Georgen, Eleanor. *The Delsarte System of Physical Culture.* New York: Butterick Publishing Co.

Stebbins, Genevieve. *Dynamic Breathing and Harmonic Gymnastics—A Complete System of Psychical, Aesthetic, and Physical Culture.* New York: E. S. Werner.

Wilbor, Elsie M., ed. *The Delsarte Recitation Book and Directory,* 2d ed., rev. and enl. New York: E. S. Werner.

1894

Foster, Joe E. *Ten Lessons in Elocution.* London: Simpkin and Marshall.

Stebbins, Genevieve. *The Delsarte System of Expression,* 5th ed. New York: E. S. Werner.

1895

Foster, Joe E. *The New Elocution.* A novel and natural method of teaching the art of elocution. London: Simpkin and Marshall.

Lowell, Marion, ed. *Harmonic Gymnastics and Pantomime Expression.* Boston: Marion Lowell. This is how it is listed in the Library of Congress Catalog. Ted Shawn says this work is often listed as having been written by Steele Mackaye.

Morgan, Anna. *An Hour with Delsarte.* Boston: Lee and Shephard.

Northrop, Henry Davenport. *Delsarte Manual of Oratory.* Cincinnati: W. H. Ferguson.

Northrop, Henry Davenport, comp. and ed. *The Delsarte Speaker; or Modern Elocution.* Designed especially for young people and amateurs. Containing a practical treatise on the Delsarte System of physical culture. Philadelphia: National Publishing Co.

Stebbins, Genevieve. *Genevieve Stebbins' Drills.* An appendix to *Society Gymnastics* containing (1) Eastern Temple Drill, (2) energizing dramatic drill, (3) minuet fan drill, and (4) an aesthetic drill. New York: E. S. Werner.

1896

Foster, Joe E. *Elocution for Children.* London: Swan Sonnenschein.

1899

Foster, Joe E. *Voice Production: Delsarte's Method.* 2d ed. Washington, Durham, Sudbury: Alfred Watson.

1901

Wilbor, Elsie M., comp. *Delsarte Recitation Book.* New York: E. S. Werner.

The Standard American Speaker and Entertainer. Recitations, headings, plays, drills, tableaux, etc. Together with rules for physical culture and for training of the voice and the use of gesture, according to the Delsarte System by Frances Putnam Pogle; also new and original musical compositions for special entertainments, etc. with many old favorites compiled and written by George M. Vickers. Entered according to Act of Congress in the year 1901 by W. E. Scull, in the Office of the Librarian of Congress, at Washington.

1902

Stebbins, Genevieve. *The Delsarte System of Expression.* 6th ed. New York: E. S. Werner.

1905

Wilbor, Elsie M., comp. *Delsarte Recitation Book.* 4th ed. enl. New York: E. S. Werner.

1910

Foster, Joe E. *Personal Magnetism.* A new source of power in delivery; founded on the Delsarte exercises. 3d ed. Washington, Durham: Alfred Watson.

1911

Foster, Joe E. *The Power of Dramatic Expression.* A book for all public speakers. London: J. F. Spriggs.

1912

Foster, Joe E. *The Delsarte Art of Preaching.* 2d ed. of *The Art of Preaching.* London: J. F. Spriggs.

Foster, Joe E. *Delsarte Aesthetic Gymnastics.* 3d. ed. London: J. F. Spriggs.

Foster, Joe E. *Lessons in Oratory; Its Theory and Practice.* 3d ed. London: J. F. Spriggs.

Foster, Joe E. *The New Elocution.* Reissue. Washington, Durham: Alfred Watson.

Foster, Joe E. *Ten Lessons in Elocution.* 2d Imp. Washington, Durham: Alfred Watson.

1913

Stebbins, Genevieve. *The Genevieve Stebbins System of Physical Training,* enl. ed. New York: E. S. Werner.

1927

O'Neill, Rose M. *The Science and Art of Speech and Gesture.* Founded on the art and life work of Delsarte with his exercises. London: C. W. Daniel.

1954

Shawn, Ted. *Every Little Movement; A Book about François Delsarte.* Pittsfield, Mass.: Eagle Printing and Binding Co.

1968

Zorn, John W., ed. *The Essential Delsarte.* Metuchen, N.J.: Scarecrow Press.

APPENDIX III

Bibliography

Ainsworth, Dorothy S. *The History of Physical Education in Colleges for Women.* New York: A. S. Barnes, 1930.

Amberg, George. *Ballet in America: The Emergence of an American Art.* New York: Mentor Books, 1949.

Barzel, Ann. "European Dance Teachers in the United States." *Dance Index* III (April-May-June 1944), 56-100.

Beaumont, Cyril W., comp. and ann. *A Bibliography of Dancing.* London: Dancing Times, 1929.

Beck, Karl. *A Treatise on Gymnastics.* Northampton, Mass.: Simeon Butler, 1828. Adapted from the writings of F. L. Jahn.

Bernheim, Alfred L., and staff of Labor Bureau. *The Business of the Theatre: An Economic History of the American Theatre 1750-1932.* New York: Benjamin Blom, 1932. Reissued 1964.

Bishop, Emily M. *Americanized Delsarte Culture.* Meadville, Pa.: Hood and Vincent, 1892.

Bode, Carl. *The Anatomy of American Popular Culture, 1840-1861.* Berkeley: University of California Press, 1959.

Bolitho, William. *Twelve Against the Gods.* New York: Viking Press, 1957. First published 1929.

Bond, Chrystelle T. "A Chronicle of Dance in Baltimore 1780-1814." *Dance Perspectives* 65 (Summer 1976).

British Museum. *General Catalogue of Published Books,* 1961.

Brown, Margaret C., and Josephine Beiderhase. "William G. Anderson." *Journal of Health, Physical Education, and Recreation* XXXI (April 1960), 34, 126.

Carson, Jane. *Colonial Virginians at Play*. Williamsburg: Colonial Williamsburg. Distributed by University Press of Virginia, Charlottesville, 1965.

Carter, Charles. "The Will of Charles Carter of Cleve." Annotated by Fairfax Harrison. *Virginia Magazine of History and Biography* XXXI (January 1923), 39-69. This will was written in September 1762.

Carter, Landon. *The Diary of Colonel Landon Carter of Sabine Hall, 1752-1778*, ed. Jack P. Greene. Charlottesville: University Press of Virginia. Published for the Virginia Historical Society, 1965.

Cheney, Sheldon. *Expressionism in Art*. New York: Liveright Publishing Corp., 1934.

Chesterfield, Philip Dormer Stanhope, Earl of. *Principles of Politeness, and of Knowing the World*. Philadelphia: Robert Bell, 1778. Evans Imprints 16077.

Christy, Arthur E., ed. *The Asian Legacy and American Life*. New York: John Day Co. 1942.

Chujoy, Anatole. *Dance Encyclopedia*. New York: A. S. Barnes, 1949.

Cohen, Selma Jeanne. "The Fourth of July, or, the Independence of American Dance." *Dance Magazine* (July 1976) 49-53.

Colby, Gertrude K. *Natural Rhythms and Dances*. New York: A. S. Barnes, 1930. First published 1922.

Cornell, Joseph, comp. "Americana: Romantic Ballet." *Dance Index* VI (1942), 204-224.

Cowley, Malcolm. *Exile's Return: A Narrative of Ideas*. New York: W. W. Norton, 1934.

Cremin, Lawrence A. *The Transformation of the School: Progressivism in American Education, 1876-1957*. New York: Vintage Books, 1961.

Davis, Elwood Craig. *The Philosophic Process in Physical Education*. Philadelphia: Lea and Febiger, 1961.

De Mille, Agnes. *Dance to the Piper*. Boston: Little, Brown, 1951.

De Morinni, Clare. "Loie Fuller, the Fairy of Light." *Dance Index* I (March 1942), 40-51.

Delaumosne, Abbé. *The Art of Oratory, System of Delsarte*, trans. Frances A. Shaw, Albany, N.Y.: E. S. Werner, 1882.

Dell, Floyd. *Were You Ever a Child?* 2d ed. New York: Knopf, 1921. First published 1919.

Delsarte System of Oratory, 3d ed. New York: E. S. Werner, 1887.

Dewey, John. *Democracy and Education*. New York: Macmillan, 1916.

————. *The School and Society*. Chicago: University of Chicago Press, 1900.

————, and Evelyn Dewey. *Schools of Tomorrow.* New York: E. P. Dutton, 1962. First published 1915.

Dickason, David Howard. *The Daring Young Men: The Story of the American Pre-Raphaelites.* Bloomington: Indiana University Press, 1953.

Dulles, Foster Rhea. *A History of Recreation: America Learns to Play,* 2d ed. New York: Appleton-Century-Crofts, 1965. First published 1940.

Duncan, Irma. "Follow Me: The Autobiography of Irma Duncan." Part I: *Dance Perspectives* 21 (1965); Part II: *Dance Perspectives* 22 (1965).

————. *Isadora Duncan: Pioneer in the Art of Dance.* New York: New York Public Library, 1959.

Duncan, Isadora. *The Art of the Dance,* ed. and with an introduction by Sheldon Cheney. New York: Theatre Arts, 1928.

————. "The Dance in Relation to Tragedy." *Theatre Arts Monthly* XI (1927), 755-761.

————. *My Life.* Garden City, N.Y.: Garden City Publishing Co., 1927.

Dzermolinska, Helen. "A Family Tree." In Doris Hering, ed. *Twenty-five Years of American Dance.* New York: Rudolf Orthwine, 1951, pp. 6-7.

Eddy, Mary Baker. *Science and Health with Key to the Scriptures.* Boston: Trustees under the will of Mary Baker Eddy. First published 1875.

Eisenberg, Emmanuel. "Ladies of the Revolutionary Dance." *New Theatre* II (February 1935), 10, 11.

Evans, Charles. *American Bibliography,* 14 vols. Chicago: Private printing for the author by the Blakely Process, 1903. Imprints of many of the works cited in the Evans bibliography are available on microfiche and are identified as Evans Imprints in this list.

Fanger, Iris M. "Boston Goes to the Ballet," *Dance Magazine* (July 1976), 47-49.

Feuillet, Raoul Auger. *Chorégraphie ou L'Art de Décrire La Dance.* Paris, 1701.

————. *Recueil de Dances.* Paris, 1704.

Fithian, Philip V. *Journal and Letters 1773-1774: A Plantation Tutor of the Old Dominion,* ed. Hunter Dickinson Farish. Williamsburg: Colonial Williamsburg, 1943.

Fletcher, Ifan Kyrle, comp. *Bibliographical Descriptions of Forty Rare Books Relating to the Art of Dancing, in the Collection of P. J. S. Richardson, O.B.E.* London: Dancing Times, 1954.

Franks, Arthur Henry. *Social Dance: A Short History.* London: Routledge and Kegan Paul, 1963.

Freedley, George. "The Black Crook and the White Fawn." *Dance Index* IV (January 1945), 4-16.

Fuller, Loie. *Fifteen Years of a Dancer's Life.* Boston: Small Maynard, 1913. Available in Dance Horizons republication.

Gallini, Giovanni Andrea. *Critical Observations on the Art of Dancing.* London, ca. 1770.

————. *A Treatise on the Art of Dancing.* London, 1772. First published 1762.

Gilfond, Henry. "Louis Horst." *Dance Observer* III (February 1936), 13.

Goldenthwaite, Vera, ed. *The Philosophy of Ingersoll.* San Francisco: Paul Elder, 1906.

Goodsell, Willystine, ed. *Pioneers of Women's Education in the United States: Emma Willard, Catherine Beecher, Mary Lyon.* New York: McGraw-Hill, 1931.

Gulick, Luther H. *The Healthful Art of Dancing.* New York: Doubleday, Page, 1910.

Guest, Ivor. *Fanny Elssler.* Middletown, Conn.: Wesleyan University Press, 1970.

————. *The Romantic Ballet in Paris.* Middletown, Conn.: Wesleyan University Press, 1966.

Hall, G. Stanley. *Educational Problems,* 2 vol. New York: Appleton, 1911.

Harris, Neil. *The Artist in American Society: The Formative Years 1790-1860.* New York: Braziller, 1966.

Hawkins, Alma M. *Modern Dance in Higher Education.* New York: Teachers College, Columbia University, 1954.

H'Doubler, Margaret. *A Manual of Dancing.* Madison, Wisc.: Tracy and Kilgore, 1921.

————. *Dance and Its Place In Education.* New York: Harcourt, Brace, 1925.

Hering, Doris, ed. *Twenty-five Years of American Dance.* New York: Rudolf Orthwine, 1951.

Hockmuth, Marie, and Richard Murphy. "Rhetorical and Elocutionary Training in Nineteenth-Century Colleges," in Karl R. Wallace, ed. *History of Speech Education in America.* New York: Appleton-Century-Crofts, 1954.

Hofstadter, Richard. *Social Darwinism in American Thought,* rev. ed. Boston: Beacon Press, 1963. First published 1944.

Hogarth, William. *The Analysis of Beauty.* Chicago: Reilly and Lee, ca. 1908. First published 1753.

Huckenpahler, Victoria. "George Washington Dances: So Agreeable and Innocent an Amusement." *Dance Magazine* (July 1976), 45-47.

Hughes, Rupert. *George Washington*, 3 vol. New York: Morrow, 1926.

Humphrey, Doris. "New Dance: An Unfinished Autobiography." *Dance Perspectives* 25 (1966).

Jaques-Dalcroze, Emile. *Eurythmics, Art and Education*, trans. Frederick Rothwell. New York: A. S. Barnes, 1930.

————. *Rhythm, Music and Education*, trans. Harold F. Rubenstein. New York: G. P. Putnam, 1921.

Keppel, Frederick P., and R. L. Duffus. *The Arts in American Life*. New York: McGraw-Hill, 1933. Published under the President's Research Committee on Social Trends.

Kieffer, Elizabeth Clarke. "John Durang, the First Native American Dancer." *The Dutchman* VI (June 1954), 26-38.

Kirstein, Lincoln. *The Book of the Dance: A Short History of Classical Theatrical Dancing*. Garden City, N.Y.: Garden City Publishing Co., 1942. First published 1935. In Dance Horizons republication with first part of title shortened to *Dance*.

Kraus, Richard. *History of the Dance in Art and Education*. Englewood Cliffs, N.J.: Prentice-Hall, 1969.

Lee, Mabel, and Bruce L. Bennett. "This Is Our Heritage: 75 Years of the American Association for Health, Physical Education and Recreation." *Journal of Health, Physical Education and Recreation* XXXI (April 1960).

Leonard, Fred Eugene. *A Guide to the History of Physical Education*, 2d ed., rev. R. Tait McKenzie. Philadelphia: Lea and Febiger, 1927.

Leuchtenburg, William E. *The Perils of Prosperity, 1914-32*. Chicago: University of Chicago Press, 1958.

Lewis, Dio. *The New Gymnastics for Men, Women and Children*. With a translation of Professor Kloss's Dumb-bell Instructor and Professor Schreber's Pangymnastikon. 3d ed. Boston: Ticknor and Fields, 1862.

"Libraries in Colonial Virginia." *William and Mary Quarterly*, 1st series, III (April 1895), 251.

Locke, John. *The Educational Writings of John Locke*, ed. James L. Axtell. Cambridge: Cambridge University Press, 1968.

MacDonald, Allan Houston. *Richard Hovey: Man and Craftsman*. Durham, N. C.: Duke University Press, 1957.

Macdougall, Allan Ross. *Isadora: A Revolutionary in Art and Love*. New York: Thomas Nelson, 1960.

Mackaye, Percy. *Epoch: The Life of Steele Mackaye, Genius of the Theatre, In Relation to His Times and Contemporaries,* 2 vols. New York: Boni and Liveright, 1927.

Magriel, Paul David. *A Bibliography of Dancing.* New York: H. W. Wilson, 1936.

―――, ed. *Isadora Duncan.* New York: Henry Holt, 1947.

Makechnie, George K. "Dudley A. Sargent." *Journal of Health, Physical Education and Recreation* XXXI (April 1960), 36, 106.

Malik, Kapila. "The Literature of Bharatanatya." *Thought* VII (August 13, 1955).

Marks, Joseph E. *America Learns to Dance: A Historical Study of Dance Education in America Before 1900.* New York: Exposition Press, 1957. Available in Dance Horizons republication.

Marsh, Agnes L., and Lucile Marsh. *The Dance in Education,* 2d ed. New York: A. S. Barnes, 1926. First published 1924.

Marsh, Lucile. "Criticizing and Critics." *American Dancer* VII (January 1934), 10.

Martin, John. *America Dancing: The Backgrounds and Personalities of the Modern Dance.* New York: Dodge Publishing Co., 1936.

Mayhew, Katherine Camp, and Anne Camp Edwards. *The Dewey School: The Laboratory School of the University of Chicago, 1896-1903.* New York: Atherton Press, 1965. First published 1936.

Maynard, Olga. *The American Ballet.* Philadelphia: Macrae Smith, 1959.

Molyneux, Anna C. "Paul Boepple and the Dalcroze School." *Dance Observer* VII (January 1940), 5.

Moore, Lillian. "The Duport Mystery." *Dance Perspectives* VII (1960).

―――. "George Washington Smith." *Dance Index* IV (June-July-August 1945), 88-135.

―――. "John Durang, the First American Dancer." *Dance Index* I (August 1942), 120-139.

―――. "Mary Ann Lee: First American Giselle." *Dance Index* II (May 1943), 60-71.

―――. *New York's First Ballet Season 1792.* New York: New York Public Library, 1961.

Morton, Louis. *Robert Carter of Nomini Hall: A Virginia Tobacco Planter of the Eighteenth Century,* 2d ed. Williamsburg: Colonial Williamsburg, 1945. First published 1941.

Nash, J. B. "Luther H. Gulick." *Journal of Health, Physical Education and Recreation* XXXI (April 1960), 60, 114.

Nietzsche, Friedrich. *Thus Spake Zarathustra,* trans. Walter Kaufmann. New York: Viking Press, 1966.

Nissen, Hartvig. *A.B.C. of the Swedish System of Educational Gymnastics.* Philadelphia: F. A. Davis, 1891.

Nye, Russel Blaine. *The Cultural Life of the New Nation, 1776-1830.* New York: Harper and Brothers, 1960.

O'Donnell, Mary P. "Margaret H'Doubler." *Dance Observer* III (November 1936), 99.

Pendennis, Peggy. "A Craze for Delsarte: Society Leaders Who Are in Love with Its Mysteries." *New York World* (August 16, 1891), p. 15.

Playford, John. *Playford's English Dancing Master.* A facsimile reprint with introduction, notes, and bibliography by Margaret Dean-Smith. London: Schott, 1957. The three volumes of Playford's work were published in many editions between 1651 and 1727. Available in Dance Horizons republication.

Poggi, Jack. *Theater in America: The Impact of Economic Forces 1870-1967.* Ithaca, N.Y.: Cornell University Press, 1968.

Radir, Ruth Anderson. *Modern Dance for the Youth of America: A Text for High School and College Teachers.* New York: Ronald Press, 1944.

Rameau, Pierre. *The Dancing Master,* trans. Cyril W. Beaumont. London: C. W. Beaumont, 1931. First edition published in Paris 1725.

Rankin, Hugh F. *The Theater in Colonial America.* Chapel Hill: University of North Carolina Press, 1960.

Rath, Emil. *Aesthetic Dancing.* New York: A. S. Barnes, 1919. First published 1914.

Ray, Harold L. "Chautauqua: Early Showcase for Physical Education." *Journal of Health, Physical Education and Recreation* XXXIII (November 1962), 37-41, 69.

Renshaw, Edyth. "Five Private Schools of Speech," in Karl R. Wallace, ed. *History of Speech Education in America.* New York: Appleton-Century-Crofts, 1954.

Riordan, William G. "Dio Lewis in Retrospect." *Journal of Health, Physical Education and Recreation* XXXI (October 1960), 47.

Robb, Mary Margaret. "The Elocutionary Movement and Its Chief Figures," in Karl R. Wallace, ed. *History of Speech Education in America.* New York: Appleton-Century-Crofts, 1954.

Rogers, Frederick Rand, ed. *Dance: A Basic Educational Technique.* New York: Macmillan, 1941.

———. *Educational Objectives of Physical Activity.* New York: A. S. Barnes, 1931.

Rousseau, Jean Jacques. *Emile; or Treatise on Education.* Abridged, trans., and ann. William H. Payne. New York: Appleton, 1914.

St. Denis, Ruth. "The Independent Art of the Dance." *Theatre Arts Monthly* VIII (June 1924), 367-372.

———. *An Unfinished Life: An Autobiography.* New York: Harper and Brothers, 1939.

Sanburn, Frederick, comp. *A Delsartean Scrap-book: Health, Personality, Beauty, House-Decoration, etc.* New York: Lovell, Gestefeld, 1890.

Saylor, Oliver M., ed. *Revolt in the Arts.* New York: Brentano, 1930.

Schlundt, Christena L. "Into the Mystic with Miss Ruth." *Dance Perspectives* 46 (Summer 1971).

———. "The 1928-29 Dance Season in New York." *The Research Quarterly* XXXIV (March 1963), 70-83. (Association for Health, Physical Education and Recreation, National Education Association.)

———. *The Professional Appearances of Ruth St. Denis and Ted Shawn: A Chronology and an Index of Dances 1906-1932.* New York: New York Public Library, 1962.

———. "The Role of Ruth St. Denis in the History of American Dance, 1906-1922." Unpublished Ph.D. dissertation, Claremont Graduate School, 1958.

Scholes, Percy Alfred. *The Puritans and Music in England and New England.* London: Oxford University Press, 1934.

Schuyler, Montgomery. *A Bibliography of the Sanskrit Drama: And an Introductory Sketch of the Dramatic Literature of India.* New York: Columbia University Press, 1906.

Seldes, Gilbert. *The Stammering Century.* New York: Harper Colophon Books, 1965. First published 1928.

Shaver, Claude L. "Steele Mackaye and the Delsartean Tradition," in Karl R. Wallace, ed. *History of Speech Education in America.* New York: Appleton-Century-Crofts, 1954.

Shawn, Ted. *The American Ballet.* New York: Henry Holt, 1926.

———. *Dance We Must.* Lectures given at Peabody College for Teachers in Nashville, June-July 1938. Pittsfield, Mass.: Ted Shawn, 1940.

———. *Every Little Movement: A Book About François Delsarte.* Pittsfield, Mass.: Eagle Printing Co., 1954. Available in Dance Horizons republication.

———, with Gray Poole. *A Thousand and One Night Stands.* Garden City, N.Y.: Doubleday, 1960.

———. *Ruth St. Denis: Pioneer and Prophet,* 2 vols. San Francisco: J. Howell, 1920.

Simpson, Claude M. *The British Broadside Ballad and Its Music.* New Brunswick, N.J.: Rutgers University Press, 1966.

Spencer, Herbert. *Education: Intellectual, Moral, and Physical.* New York: Appleton, 1898. First published 1860.

Spiesman, Mildred. "Creative Dance in American Life and Educa-

tion." Unpublished D.Ed. project, Teachers College, Colum-
bia University, 1949.
Staley, S. C., and D. M. Lowery. *Manual of Gymnastic Dancing.* New
York: Association Press, 1920.
Stanard, W. G. "Major Robert Beverley and His Descandants." *Vir-
ginia Magazine of History and Biography* III (April 1896),
383-392.
Stebbins, Genevieve. *The Delsarte System of Expression,* 6th ed. New
York: E. S. Werner, 1902. First published 1885. Available in
Dance Horizons republication.
―――. *Dynamic Breathing and Harmonic Gymnastics: A Complete System
of Psychical, Aesthetic and Physical Culture.* New York: E. S.
Werner, 1893.
―――. *The Genevieve Stebbins System of Physical Training.* Enl. ed. New
York: E. S. Werner, 1913. First published 1898.
―――. *Society Gymnastics and Voice Culture.* New York: E. S. Werner,
1888.
Terry, Walter. *Ballet: A New Guide to the Liveliest Art.* New York: Dell,
1959.
―――. *Miss Ruth: The More Living Life of Ruth St. Denis.* New York:
Dodd, Mead, 1969.
Van Cleef, Joy. "Rural Felicity: Social Dance in 18th-Century Con-
necticut." *Dance Perspectives* 65 (Spring 1976).
Van Dalen, Deobold B., Elmer D. Mitchell, and Bruce L. Bennet. *A
World History of Physical Education: Cultural, Philosophical, Com-
parative.* Englewood Cliffs, N.J.: Prentice-Hall, 1953.
Verwer, Hans. *Guide to the Ballet,* trans. Henry Mins. New York:
Barnes and Noble, 1936.
Wagner, Richard. *Wagner on Music and Drama: A Compendium of
Richard Wagner's Prose Works,* ed. Albert Goldman and Evert
Sprinchorn; trans. H. Ashton Ellis. New York: E. P. Dutton,
1964.
Wallace, Karl R., ed. *History of Speech Education in America.* New York:
Appleton-Century-Crofts, 1954.
Washington, George. *The Diaries of George Washington, 1748-1799,* 4
vols., ed. John C. Fitzpatrick. Boston: Houghton Mifflin, 1925.
Published for the Mount Vernon Ladies Association of the
Union.
Weiss, David. "Isadora Duncan . . . Actress: And Her Influence on
the Theater." *Dance Magazine* XXXIV (February 1960), 40-43,
74-75.
*Werner's Directory of Elocutionists, Readers, Lecturers, and Other Public
Instructors and Entertainers,* ed. Elsie M. Wilbor. New York:
E. S. Werner, 1887.

White, Morton. *Social Thought in America: The Revolt Against Formalism*. Boston: Beacon Press, 1957. First published 1949.

Whitehead, Walter Muir. *The Arts in Early American History*, with bibliography by Wendell D. Garrett and Jane N. Garrett. Chapel Hill: University of North Carolina Press. Published for the Institute of Early American History and Culture at Williamsburg, Va., 1965.

Whitman, Walt. *Leaves of Grass*. New York: Mentor Books, 1954. First published 1854.

Who's Who in America, ed. John W. Leonard. Chicago: A. N. Marquis, 1899 *et seq.*

Winter, Marian Hannah. "American Theatrical Dancing from 1750 to 1800." *Musical Quarterly* XXIV (January 1938), 58-73.

————. "Augusta Maywood." *Dance Index* II (January-February 1943), 4-19.

Wright, Louis B. *The Cultural Life of the American Colonies, 1607-1763*. New York: Harper Torchbooks, 1962. First published 1957.

Wright, Louis B., George B. Tatum, John W. McCoubrey, and Robert C. Smith. *The Arts in America: The Colonial Period*. New York: Scribner's, 1966.

Wynne, Shirley. "From Ballet to Ballroom: Dance in the Revolutionary Era." *Dance Scope* X (Fall-Winter 1975-1976), 65-73.

Zorn, John W., ed. *The Essential Delsarte*. Metuchen, N.J.: Scarecrow Press, 1968.

INDEX

Index

Entries with page numbers in brackets refer to illustrations.